Benyamin Chetkow-Yanoov, DSW

Celebrating Diversity
Coexisting
in a Multicultural Society

Pre-publication
REVIEWS,
COMMENTARIES,
EVALUATIONS . . .

"*Celebrating Diversity* makes a valuable contribution to peace theory and practice. Chetkow-Yanoov addresses the complex causes of conflict in civil societies—racism, oppression, and intergroup rivalry. This book looks to positive examples from Canada, Holland, Israel, Namibia, and the United States to cite strategies to help diverse groups live together with respect in a pluralist society. The author provides useful examples of how citizens can become politicians and engage in organized protest and ways that professionals can empower citizens to take action to correct many of the injustices that cause violence throughout the postmodern world."

Ian Harris, EdD
Executive Secretary, Peace Education Committee, International Peace Research Association; Professor, Department of Educational Policy and Community Studies, University of Wisconsin, Milwaukee

"*This* book is timely and valuable. It makes a convincing case for why traditional establishment-minority relations, based on either segregation or integration, are doomed to failure; and why cultural diversity, based on participation and coexistence, is not only about being politically correct, but offers the best long-run protection from the violence and conflict that threaten contemporary societies.

The book succeeds extraordinarily well in doing what it promises to do—prepare for coexistence in a pluralist society. It first familiarizes the reader with basic concepts and approaches, then moves to building the tools, and finally taking action. It is interspersed with practical suggestions and an impressive range of examples of policies and practices of coexistence at all levels of the social structure—national, community, organizational, and the group. Written in a friendly style, this is a satisfying book for the intelligent reader who wants both the findings from academic research and practical solutions based on decades of accumulated experience in making cultural diversity work.

This is an optimistic, but by no means naive, book about what society could be like if only more of us would 'play fair,' 'clean up our own mess,' and 'hold hands and stick together.' It is a thoughtful book that offers multiple options for how to achieve the goals of coexistence in diversity."

Dafna Nundi Izraeli, PhD
Professor of Sociology and Department Chair, Bar-Ilan University, Israel

Celebrating Diversity
Coexisting
in a Multicultural Society

Celebrating Diversity
Coexisting
in a Multicultural Society

Benyamin Chetkow-Yanoov, DSW

The Haworth Press
New York • London

The Haworth Press, Inc., 10 Alice Street, Binghamton, NY 13904-1580

Cover design by Monica L. Seifert.

The Library of Congress has cataloged the hardcover edition of this book as:

Chetkow-Yanoov, B.
    Celebrating diversity : coexisting in a multicultural society / Benyamin Chetkow-Yanoov.
        p.   cm.
    Includes biographical references and index.
    ISBN 0-7890-0437-2 (alk. paper).
    1. Pluralism (Social sciences). 2. Social integration. I. Title.
HM131.C7142 1999
301—dc21
                                                                98-41559
                                                                    CIP

ISBN 0-7890-0438-0 (pbk.)

Good ideas are really fine,
but implementation is divine.

ABOUT THE AUTHOR

Benyamin Chetkow-Yanoov, DSW, is a retired professor of community social work. He continues to engage in professional teaching and consultation in Israel. Dr. Chetkow-Yanoov has also pioneered undergraduate and graduate courses in conflict-resolution. The author of *Social Work Approaches to Conflict Resolution: Making Fighting Obsolete* and *Social Work Practice: A Systems Approach* (Second Edition, Haworth), he has served as a consultant for a Jerusalem project to prepare community volunteers for doing neighborhood conflict resolution. He has participated in the creation of four peace curricula for public schools in Israel, and one such curriculum for the public schools in Holland. His professional interests include the dynamics of program implementation, volunteerism, conflict resolution, social planning, and successful aging. Dr. Chetkow-Yanoov's current efforts include developing a project of networking among Israeli coexistence organizations (for the Abraham Fund), and teaching the conflict-resolution message at various international and local conferences. In past years, he contributed to intergroup dialogue between Palestinians and Israelis as well as between Jewish leftists and rightists.

CONTENTS

Figures and Tables

Figures

Chapter 7

Tables

Chapter 4

Chapter 8

Foreword

This book is a remarkable guide for those who strive for coexistence among individuals, groups, and subcultures in our pluralist diverse society. Professor Benyamin Chetkow-Yanoov believes that we can overcome tensions and conflicts in our society by creating structured dialogue among ourselves. The basis for any decision is conceptual, and the choice we have to make is between two extreme concepts—segregation and coexistence. Government and voluntary organizations should choose coexistence if they are interested in the prevention or reduction of tensions and conflicts.

Being an experienced social work educator and a strong believer in community organization, the author suggests that social action is the right strategy to create community readiness for coexistence. The reader can benefit from the review of basic principles for coexistence, learn from worldwide examples, or follow the exercises at the end of each chapter. The book is recommended to educators who are interested in designing curricula for coexistence.

Aric Rimmerman
Dean, Faculty of Social Welfare
and Health Studies
University of Haifa

Preface

During the late 1960s and the early 1970s, as citizens of the United States, my wife and I became involved in the community life of an inner-city neighborhood of Indianapolis. We started by opposing the blockbusting activities of unscrupulous real estate agencies who exploited our gradual shift from an all-white to a mixed (white-black) area. As we got to know and work with our new African-American neighbors, we found ourselves deep into a new type of experience—forming a new neighborhood association and cooperating with people who were different from us. Together, former strangers groped toward what is now called "coexistence." Spiritually, this was a very challenging time for us.

Then, feeling a desire for closeness to cultural roots, our family moved to Israel in 1971. We settled in a small all-Jewish city, and lived the lives of new immigrants for the next few years—once again amidst unfamiliar surroundings. We began to learn about our country's internal and external tensions, especially in connection to the Yom Kippur war in 1973. We were troubled to notice deep Jewish fears, and expectations of future wars.

A very few years later, Egypt's President Sadat suddenly visited Israel. He shattered all our stereotypes when he made his dramatic plea for peace in the Israeli parliament. We became aware of the Arab (today, Palestinian) citizens of Israel, and that we knew nothing about them. We had never met an Arab socially.

Slowly during the 1980s, we became activists in the field of Arab-Jewish relations. We discovered that our earlier experiences in Indianapolis were very helpful—and we began again to rediscover the excitement of learning to coexist with people who were different from us. Interestingly, the intercultural association in which we spent the next eleven years was called "Partnership."

In Israel today, I find many persons searching for coexistence skills in a variety of human endeavors. It seems advisable to bring a coexistence or partnership approach to the continuing hostility between people of rightist versus leftist political persuasions; between religious and secular Jews; between Israelis and Palestinians; and between others who are adhering to rigidly dichotomized stands.

When I see many of us learning to outgrow our earlier stereotypic ways of handling our ignorance about, and fear of, the unknown "other," I feel optimistic. I hope this book proves helpful to new colleagues in the coexistence field. We would do well to remember that in a coexistence society, there are no strangers.

Benyamin Chetkow-Yanoov, DSW

Acknowledgments

This book owes much to the efforts of two creative librarians who helped me gather materials from all over the world and to diverse colleagues who made the effort to write me about recent developments in their countries. I have been helped by some very talented computer experts to overcome my ignorance of machines and to use electronic means to get my writing done.

I especially thank my African-American and Arab-Palestinian friends for their patience and for their readiness to take risks along with me as we explored new paradigms and intervention modes. Many grassroots persons and technical experts have guided me along new paths toward coexistence.

As in all my other publications, I am indebted to my wife Bracha for editing the text and for her many creative suggestions for improving it.

Chapter 1

Preparing for Life in a Pluralist World

INTRODUCTION

Elites and Out-Groups

For many centuries, human beings have lived according to a paradigm of elitism, privilege, or chosenness—especially when they enjoyed physical and ethnic homogeneity. This was often based on the religious, linguistic, social, and cultural characteristics of the group into which one was born. Ideally, membership in such a group gave one a sense of personal-clan-family identity, loyalty to ancestors, history, tradition, and behavioral norms. Awareness of joint suffering, pride in the group's achievements, and commitments to mutual aid enhanced group cohesion.

Unfortunately, ethnicity can also be the basis for building walls between (or segregating) ethnic groups. Many prophets, kings, priests, and heads of prestigious family clans translated ethnic or racial identity into the certainty that one's own group is unique and morally better than all the others. Such values often justified exploiting members of out-groups and avoiding contamination by "strangers" or low-caste subordinates. The outcome was usually racist elitism—which marginalized or victimized members of other "undeserving" groups. In fact, belonging to a rejected ethnic group may fill its members with shame or self-hatred (Lewin, 1948; Lewis and Keung, 1975; Rouhana and Bar-Tel, 1998).

Another type of elitism was based on the control of wealth and power. The wealthy rejected the poor (often defined as members of a socially inferior or unworthy ethnic group), using them for society's menial jobs. In situations of power symmetry, rival kings or emperors tended to be courteous to each other—while viewing the poor as basically disreputable. Over long periods of time, outcasts such as the Jews or the Gypsies survived if they were quiet. Those who rebelled were conquered, enslaved, exiled, or eliminated.

Today, establishments (e.g., power structures, military-ruled countries) are accepted as appropriate norm setters, controllers of available resources, makers of policy, and authorizers of implementation and enforcement, as well as determiners of the rules of the power game itself (Hunter, 1953). In most countries, local norms sanction a reality in which those who do not belong have little status, few resources, meager services, and only a subsistence lifestyle.

Accordingly, persons or groups who are clearly different from the establishment are considered deviant. In some cases, these strangers are thought to pose a threat to the ruling elite. Consequently, this out-group "deserves" to be rejected or controlled. Its inferiority or inadequacy is prejudged, having little to do with standards of behavior, effectiveness in performing specific roles, or whether the group constitutes a large or small percentage of the local population (Chetkow-Yanoov, 1997; Kosmin, 1979; Kung, 1962; Lewis and Keung, 1975).

The very structure of such a world has influenced our thinking in one significant way—we conceive of the universe in dichotomous terms. For example: light and dark, good and evil, yin and yang, women and men, Jews and Gentiles, Catholics and heretics, Greeks and barbarians. Dichotomization continues in distinctions between the third world and the West, blacks or whites,

Croats or Serbs, Tutsis or Hutus, Republicans or Democrats, etc. Such a paradigm is convenient for continuing the privileges of members of local and national elites.

Living in an Increasingly Pluralist Reality

Significant technological changes (such as the printing press, electricity, the telephone, television, and computers) have increased the mobility of people all over this planet during the past 100 years. The invention of steam-driven trains, the automobile, and inexpensive air travel also contributed to significant changes. The spread of democratic government, efflorescence of the middle class, urbanization, Einstein's theory of relativity, change in the roles played by women, the relaxation of many of the world's geographic boundaries, and the increase of aged/retired populations are examples of what has been happening at a very rapid pace all over the world.

In fact, the world seems to be getting smaller every day. Public institutions, metropolitan areas, even entire countries seem less and less homogeneous. Most countries have, in fact, become transformed from one-culture societies into ethnically, religiously, or linguistically pluralistic ones—as has happened, for example, between the French and English speakers in Canada. Terms such as multiculturalism, pluralism, or diversity have become popular, and remind us that we might do well to avoid previous generations' absolutist outlooks and rigid categories. Figure 1.1 helps us define reality flexibly.

Our newly possible contacts with many cultures or peoples is seen more and more as enriching. The operation of the European Common Market, and of the United Nations itself, seems to exemplify the heterogeneity of today's world. We no longer go to the "Far" East—as if Europe were the center of the world; instead, we travel to Thailand or Japan.

Figure 1.1. What Is Reality?

"The topic for today is: What is reality?"

Many former ethnic or cultural (minority) groups are no longer willing to postpone the satisfying of their basic needs, be exploited economically, or to assimilate (Mitchell, 1990). Cults and fundamentalist believers continue to flourish, but the world's religions are learning to cooperate on matters of overall spiritual concern. As exemplified by developments in Rwanda, a national-cultural identity (or peoplehood) often is not synonymous with citizenship in a geographic country (Gurr, 1993; Hoffman, 1982). If their identity is challenged or threatened these days, minority peoples such as the Armenians or Basques tend to react violently.

After centuries of elitist rule, we find serious "minority-majority" conflicts in such diverse countries as Belgium, Canada,

Cambodia, Germany, India, Iraq, Ireland, Israel, Liberia, Rwanda, Spain, South Africa, the former Yugoslavia, the United States, and the former Soviet Union. The lot of Gypsy, Asian, or black population groups is still difficult throughout the Western world. In light of the disruptive and costly consequences of continuing a "separate and unequal" policy, business as usual is becoming very risky.

As humankind prepares to enter the twenty-first century, it becomes urgent that leaders and professional disciplines develop new basic concepts or paradigms and find ways to set them into operation. *Coexistence* is one such paradigm. Accordingly, ethnic groups now become "separate and equal." While continuing to honor their ethnic or national identities, our planet's social units also become world citizens. For example, both the Dutch and the Jews, who are small in numbers and speak a very particular language, have had to become multilingual to get along in the world. In fact, during its golden age in the seventeenth century, tolerance of others and coexistence with different cultures became a cornerstone of Dutch culture. The works of Erasmus and Spinoza opened Dutch culture to other Europeans without losing any of its uniqueness or identity. An equivalent process took place for the Jews during the French enlightenment in the eighteenth century, before the emergence of the Zionist movement.

The idea of tolerance (i.e., acceptance of others unlike oneself) is not to be associated with weakness or permissiveness. Living together with respect for one another, despite our differences, requires emotional strength, patience, learning, even bravery. It is also based on everyone respecting and keeping the law—so that our efforts can be made in a stable social setting.

The survival of small countries such as Holland or Denmark, in the teeth of powerful environmental pressures to assimilate into, say, the European Union, presents another facet of the issue. Preserving language alternatives in the public schools of multicultural societies (as is done in some North American and European countries) seems one of the steps toward celebrating diversity and making coexistence operational in the twenty-first century (Chetkow-Yanoov, 1997; Gurr, 1993).

PURPOSE OF THIS BOOK

This book focuses on the essential requirements of a workable, twenty-first century, urban, culturally pluralistic coexistence society (see definitions in Chapter 3). My intention is not only to identify some of the basic elements of a functioning coexistence society but also to design some first steps for implementing these basic elements within a period of perhaps five years (Boulding, 1988). If this effort can devise something workable, the product might serve as a model for many countries.*

Hawaii, Holland, and Israel are appropriate places in which to test some of these coexistence ideas. These are pluralistic, highly urban, multilingual environments, yet they remain essentially different from one another. They are representative of a trend toward pluralism on the global scene. Much might also be learned from looking at current developments in Canada, Namibia, or Switzerland. It is safe to hypothesize that, despite the cultural diversity of these six places, their multiculturalism might have significant elements in common.

---

* Hopefully, the book will also provide a basis for specific curriculum manuals for children from grades nine to twelve. A parallel study manual could be readied for the parents of children learning multiculturalism. Materials could also be prepared for training the teachers who are to communicate the program in their classrooms. I think it is important to create such teaching materials as a partial antidote to the ethnic violence that is erupting all over our planet. Ignorance and suspicion of strangers must be transformed into operational skills for meeting, understanding, and getting along with people unlike ourselves.

The project requires that we first explore and clarify a number of theoretic concepts and issues. These will be supplemented with detailed case examples from various countries, especially countries that show a transition from segregation to coexistence.

FOCUS OF THE BOOK'S CONTENTS

Chapter 1 begins with a look at examples of intergroup pluralism today, and it outlines my growing interest in the subject.

Chapter 2 explores two recognized approaches to intergroup relations: segregation (or separation and coercive control of minority groups) and integration (or the assimilation of minority groups into the majority culture). The advantages and disadvantages of both paths are explored.

Chapter 3 focuses on the nature and requirements of coexistence—in which diverse cultures flourish side by side in a pluralist society. This approach is seen as essential for life on this planet in the twenty-first century.

Chapter 4 examines various types of deliberate social action which might help us move from preserving the status quo to a readiness for a coexistence reality—including protest, activating grassroots or citizen groups, advocacy, and lobbying.

Chapter 5 describes educational efforts for coexistence that are judged to be successful. It will analyze some of the factors that helped these efforts succeed. I also suggest a number of ways for bringing about coexistence in culturally mixed societies. Both governmental and voluntary/citizen efforts will be described and related to each other.

Chapter 6 presents coexistence efforts of five different countries and looks at the implications for achieving positive results everywhere.

Chapter 7 suggests a number of relevant topics worthy of further research attention.

Chapter 8 deals with implications of the book's theme and its findings. Recommendations are made for the next operational and policy-level steps.

SUMMARY

Our planetary history includes, alas, many examples of elitist control of large population groups—usually accompanied by the elite's biases (e.g., racism) and exploitation of outsiders. This book focuses on some subsequent developments—that is, the shift from culturally homogeneous societies to pluralistic ones.

By the end of the twentieth century, cultural diversity is becoming a legitimate part of social policy. The ways of segregation and integration are proving bankrupt. In many countries, gradual interest is being shown in the idea of coexistence and in learning skills, values, and theories which would help us move in that direction. Pride and assertiveness (about one's culture) remain crucial for everybody, but do not necessarily lead to controlling or downgrading others. To accomplish this change nonviolently, new curricula are being created and taught to schoolteachers, to pupils, and to their families.

EXERCISES

What Can We Learn from History?

Compare and contrast the lot of any two ethnic populations (e.g., blacks in America and those in South Africa, the Gypsies and the Jews) during this century's transition from elitist to more democratic types of society.

Getting to Know Your Neighbors

Have you met personally with individual members of a minority group in your country? If yes, in what circumstances did you meet?

If you have never met any representatives of the minority groups in your region, would meeting with such persons enrich or complicate your life? Why do you think so? What could you do to change your present situation?

Chapter 2

Three Archaic Patterns
of Establishment–Minority Relations

INTRODUCTION

Since elites still tend to treat their minorities shabbily, and healthy members of minority groups resent being rejected or exploited, intergroup conflicts can be observed all over this planet. Few self-respecting groups are satisfied to be segregated unjustly or merely to be tolerated. They are also unwilling to integrate into the host society in order to receive equal rights. If those in control continue doing business as it has been done over the past centuries, more and more conflicts will erupt, and most of them will escalate into serious violence.

In this chapter, we will look at four basic generators of conflict. We will find that these four variables provide a basis for analyzing the nature of segregation, tolerance, and integration as well as provide us with clues about overcoming their social limitations.

FOUR CAUSES OF CONFLICT

In the following material, I suggest that four components or causal factors are part of any ongoing conflict relationship (Chetkow-Yanoov, 1996). It is hypothesized that all conflicts, from the smallest to the largest, include these four essential components (see Figure 2.1).

Figure 2.1. Four Components of All Conflicts

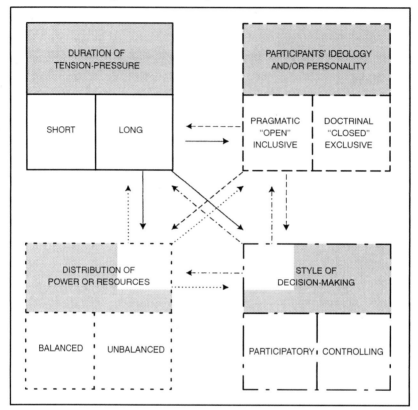

Duration of Tension/Pressure

Example: In a slum neighborhood of Rio de Janeiro, constant tension and lack of resources have broken up many impoverished families. Parents turn to hard drugs, and children run away from home to live in the streets. A life of constant crisis and frustration leave the children little to hope for. Their ability to cope with problems is further reduced by illiteracy and a desperate need for immediate satisfactions. To survive, the boys resort to petty crime and the girls to prostitution—inevitably getting into trouble with the police. Even if they could sit still in the local school, these street children are not welcome in the middle-class social services available to their street and neighborhood.

Continuing conditions of pressure and/or tension in the environment cause many people to feel serious discomfort. As situational demands exceed their capacity to manage, their activity diminishes, and their mutual support networks cease to function. In such situations, individuals or groups may cease to interact with their environment, causing them to experience a crisis that they find overwhelming.

Crisis is usually of limited duration. In other words, people in crisis might feel depressed or inadequate for, say, a few months, and then begin to recover (as they do after mourning the loss of a loved one). The problem is complicated when the crisis situation persists for a long period of time and/or relevant services (e.g., hot line counseling) do not exist. Persons or groups under continuous tension for long periods usually experience physical and mental exhaustion, burnout, and (because of coping poorly) more tension.

In such situations, ruling elite members tend to defend themselves by simplifying the world into dichotomous camps (e.g., "we" versus "them") or behaving with the certainty that "all the world is against us." As they become more and more polarized, they tend to rely on a power base domination style of decision-making, and on segregation of minority groups.

Closed Personality and/or Ideology of the Participants

Example: In central Africa, where the Tutsi and Hutu peoples have been victimizing each other for some 200 years (often accompanied by feelings of humiliation, fear, and rage), both groups became fanatically closed-minded. When some incident precipitated a crisis, the situation erupted into violence that resembled a holocaust. Being forced to flee into temporary refugee camps added more fuel to the emotional fire.

Incidents of violent ethnic cleansing, such as the Serb-Croat confrontations in the Yugoslavia region, have been uncovered. Some news media reports stressed that perpetrators of such atrocities felt completely justified in taking revenge on those who had done them evil in the recent past.

Long-lasting interpersonal or international conflicts are often accompanied by a change from pragmatic, inclusive, humor-filled, decentralized, open behavior to a devotion to purity of ideology or principles, centralization, seriousness, and elitism. Participants in an ongoing or escalating conflict often experience a drying up of communication from outside their identity groups.

In recent history, such closed behavior is exemplified by the action style of the Ayatollah Khomeini (in Iran). Similarly, when the very conservative Barry Goldwater was a candidate for the presidency of the United States, he came up with the slogan "Better Dead Than Red." In closed persons or systems, alternatives disappear and even bystanders must choose "for me or against me." Generally, the situation worsens if the participants are also uninformed, thus relying on rumors, generalizations, and stereotypes.

Closed human groups tend to function in a decidedly self-righteous style, to dominate decision making, and to exclude others as unworthy of consideration. When they also have a large amount of power, they can rationalize the use of violence against a persistent opponent or a troublesome minority group.

Distribution of Power and Influence

Example: In a certain nickel-rich part of eastern Canada, the provincial government made a deal with an international corporation to develop this resource. The corporation was willing to allocate a percentage of expected profits to the provincial government, but neither the politicians nor the business executives seemed ready to make any kind of deal with members of a First Nation (aboriginal) tribe, who technically own the land in question. The latter (long considered a weak group whose opinion is not important) objected to being bypassed economically. They brought the entire development process to a halt by starting a legal process in the courts and by threatening massive protests at the site of the proposed mine.

Scholars such as Lingas (1988) or Weingarten and Leas (1987) emphasize the centrality of power in continuing conflictual relations. The course of most conflicts is influenced by competition for power, influence, or resources (e.g., for control over the water of a river or a natural resource such as oil). In addition, Purnell (1988) and Eisler (1987) stress the differences between power arrangements that are symmetric (all rivals are of similar strength; power is shared) and those which are not (one side is very strong, the others weak). They stipulate that the more asymmetric the power situation, the more likely that a conflict will escalate toward violence.

In the days of the great empires, the strong ruled and the weak were conquered and exploited. Even today, a powerful elite can control things paternalistically or manipulate its subordinates openly. During the twentieth century, powerful closed-minded elites have spawned genocidal "events" in Nazi Germany, Cambodia, and Rwanda (Fattah, 1981). However, having the power to win wars, or to dominate family arguments, is not enough to guarantee peace. The loser's acquiescence may be brief and certainly does not create trusting relationships. If the strong party is too oppressive, members of the dominated side may, in their bitterness and humiliation, become obsessed with a desire for revenge. Such has been the case for Israelis and Palestinians in the Middle East, the Serbs and Croats in the Balkans, or the Tutsis and Hutus in Central Africa.

Power arrangements are central to the discussion of segregation and coexistence addressed later in this chapter.

Style of Decision Making

Example: In a number of long-neglected neighborhoods of an American metropolis, a new federal-state urban renewal program changed conditions dramatically. Small areas that had been neglected by city hall and the ruling political party became full partners in decision making about their communities, and local citizens had to make up 50 percent of the neighborhood committees. Instead of being told what to do by a precinct official, they were trained to organize meetings and to conduct sessions democratically. A few years later, these locally trained and experienced neighborhood leaders began to appear as elected members of the city council.

Authoritarian use of power does achieve quick results, but it also generates resentment, exacerbates dichotomies, and contributes to the intensification of a conflict. This stance is rooted in suspicion, fear, contempt, and secrecy—the usual conditions for attaining obedience. Oligarchic privilege often masks racist exploitation and bureaucratic manipulation.

On the other hand, widening opportunities for rivals to participate in decision making or to enjoy mutual benefits (e.g., in food-buying cooperatives, interdisciplinary committees, or multiparty coalitions) constitute a sound basis for cooperation and mutuality (Chetkow-Yanoov, 1986). The participatory style is easily accompanied by ideological openness, shared power arrangements (i.e., empowering of the weaker side), and a readiness to coexist with others in a complex world (Shera and Page, 1995).

IMPLICATIONS OF ASYMMETRIC
POWER ARRANGEMENTS

In a classic example of power-influence asymmetry, the minority group can do little to improve its image in the eyes of the establishment. Its members are often characterized as follows:

- Different, nonnormative, strange
- Morally inferior, primitive, not human
- Fit only for doing society's dirty jobs
- Undeserving of consideration or rights
- Unclean, evil, corrupting, dangerous

Again, these judgments are not based on empirical facts. They are part of a continuing ignorance about the true nature of the minority group.

The elite's coercive behavior is often rooted in an unrecognized fear of the very downtrodden population it is exploiting. In the days of historic colonial empires, this ideology served as justification for exploiting weak groups or nations; based on perverted Darwinism, religious credos such as "the white man's burden," and early capitalism's need for cheap labor and captive consumer populations.

In the past, weak, stigmatized, or isolated groups were forced to conform to the desires of the controlling establishment. Sometimes they overidentified with the aggressors, trying to behave like them. Today, because growing literacy and access to television have made oppressed groups aware of what they are missing, they are much less conformist. They often are so angered at their continuing victimization that, similar to the people in Northern Ireland, African-American residents of Los Angeles, or the Basques in Spain, their rage turns into civic or international violence (Danieli, 1985).

Toward the end of the twentieth century, former victimizers and exploiters are experiencing serious challenges from their previously unassertive minority populations.

THREE PATTERNS OF RELATING TO STRANGERS IN OUR MIDST

Segregation

Over the past few thousand years, one of the basic patterns of interaction between strong and weak groups has been segregation of the weak or minority groups. In segregated societies, bigoted values make for legal and physical isolation of designated minority groups. Usually this means that the elite group lives well, while dominated groups are neglected, dehumanized, rejected, and victimized. The powerful often use segregation as a vehicle for dividing, conquering, and exploiting others (Anda, 1984; Chetkow-Yanoov, 1996). Minority groups usually have significantly fewer public and social services, and the few existing ones are of poor quality. Their members must compete harder for jobs, as well as for common amenities, than do majority-group persons.

Members of nonestablishment groups are placed in stereotyped categories that allow for few exceptions. This may well lead to enforced group ghettoization. As mentioned previously, continuing victimization leads to a rising tide of rage, terrorism, and backlash (Grier and Cobbs, 1968). Today, subscribing to the segregation model becomes more and more expensive for the local establishment—as England and Israel have learned the hard way in Ireland and in the Middle East, and the Afrikaners discovered in South Africa. The elitist-segregationist stance continues to be the driving force behind many contemporary intra- and international wars.

Martinez (1997) illustrates these conditions in her description of the Mexican-American experience in a U.S. public school system. First, members of the dominant group argue about the way to label the student—Hispanic, Chicano/a, La Raza (the American Indian and African roots of most Hispanics are overlooked). The pupils continue to be immigrants, no matter how long they have lived in the United States. As "children of color" in a school, the pupils are also made to feel like freaks among the whites. Names are anglicized (e.g., Estivan becomes Steve), disapproval of the Spanish language is widespread, and Mexican history or culture are invisible in the curriculum. There is equally little attention to the history of American genocide of native peoples during the expansion southward and westward. Chicano teachers are rare in the school system. Martinez is not surprised that a very low percentage of Chicano youth finish high school, but she suggests that they are "push outs," not dropouts.

Even when an oppressed minority cannot fight back directly, it does not necessarily lapse into shame and apathy. It often compensates for the harshness of reality by developing a sense of being an unrecognized actual or spiritual elite (Kosmin, 1979). If members of an exploited population eventually win freedom and come to power without dealing with their accumulated rage in a healthy way, their thirst for vengeance may cause them to scapegoat others even more harshly than they had been scapegoated in their own past (Shamir and Sullivan, 1985). The cost to everyone is very high.

In summary, a segregated society invests heavily in policing, social control, and the need for enemies (Harkabi, 1972; Volkan, 1988; Wahlstrom, 1989). It will be stable, organized, and (as in fascist Italy) the trains will run on time. Its decision making will be centralized, authoritarian, and fast. In it, strangers are controlled, exploited, or eliminated. However, when its minority groups are no longer isolated or illiterate, they tend to rebel, and their escalating opposition often leads to terror and counter-violence.

With the rapid spread of traditional and electronic literacy, more and more people are discovering an actual pluralism in their countries (Hoffman, 1982; Samooha, 1978). Although former underdogs still explode into violent rebellion, and bigotry still characterizes relations between adherents of various religions, the "times they are a-changin'." Concerned people all over this planet have come to question the wisdom of continuing with a paradigm that seems bankrupt. Some new paradigms seem necessary to escape from centuries of bigoted colonialism and to get free of past rage-filled we (good) versus them (evil) dichotomies (Chetkow-Yanoov, 1997). Scholars and practitioners have begun searching for a new conceptual model. One new paradigm for moving in such a direction (e.g., integration) is described in a following section, and another (coexistence) is analyzed in Chapter 3.

Tolerance

According to my engineering colleagues, tolerance means how much a specific kind of metal might be bent (back and forth) before it breaks or shatters into pieces. In social terms, the concept usually indicates the willingness of an establishment culture to accept strangers into its midst (without resorting to segregation or violence). In the tolerant society, outsiders are not harmed, might be excluded only partially, and are not required to assimilate. The local elite finds that "putting up with" outgroups is lucrative.

In fact, a considerable measure of tolerance is essential to the success of any program of integration (see next section). The lack of actual tolerance among the various Jewish ethnic groups of Israel explains the failure of an integration effort in its junior high schools (Amir, Sharan, and Ben-Ari, 1984). Obviously, a foundation of tolerance is also essential for the success of any program of coexistence (see Chapter 3).

Integration

In this alternative to segregation, the establishment group remains much stronger than any of the minority ones. Under conditions of relative self-confidence, and often backed with moral ideals, some establishment's leaders start to tolerate those who are different. The elite makes deliberate efforts to attract minority populations "into its bosom"—that is, to demand they resocialize or acculturate into the ruling culture. Former strangers are expected to shed much of their cultural uniqueness (i.e., to become deculturated) and to assimilate into the majority culture —as happened among the nineteenth-century Irish, Italian, and Jewish immigrants in the United States.

Actually, the majority group often absorbs some minority-culture characteristics into its way of life. By becoming so enriched, it also becomes more similar to the minority group it is trying to absorb. On the other hand, the uniqueness and strangeness of the weak group is expected to disappear over a reasonable period of time—under what has been called "pressure cooker" conditions (Watts and Hughes, 1964; Samooha, 1978; Young, 1967).

At first, integration results in both groups modifying or discarding some of their former characteristics, gradually becoming more and more like each other (Rich, Amir, and Ben-Ari, 1981). The ultimate outcome is that all groups eventually merge into a new homogeneity. In theory, integration is supposed to improve the lot of the minority group. As it becomes more and more like the majority, its members qualify for the same rights as everyone else. Actually, integration may destroy the informal network of mutual aid previously typical of minority-group society. It may cause members of the minority group to experience serious problems of identity, a sense of loss, and feelings of anger.

Self-respecting members of the minority group usually try to maintain their uniqueness despite the temptations that integration poses. They tend to marry only persons of their own group, send their children to private (ethnic) day schools, and keep certain ceremonies in private (Antonovsky, 1960; Clark, 1990; Eaton, 1952; Sklare, 1958). Minority persons often develop a special kind of humor that pokes fun at themselves and also at the majority group (in acceptable ways).

Since an integrated society aims for the tranquillity of homogeneity, it will have to invest heavily in education and resocialization services. Its decision making is based on normative consensus and may be rather slow. Strangers (often immigrants) are seen as raw material to be put into the societal pressure cooker so that their uniqueness can be shed as quickly as possible. Such a society may also tend toward minimal risk taking, or conservatism.

TOLERANCE AND INTEGRATION ARE NOT ENOUGH

Integration does seem an enormous improvement over continued segregation. It is based on an expanded sense of tolerance (as shown in Figure 2.2).

However, tolerance is seen as something that a well-meaning establishment does condescendingly (and often reluctantly). Integration, on the other hand, has a much more positive image. It is usually based on a policy of absorption (e.g., of migrants or war refugees), persuasion, and education. Its advocates, claiming that integration makes for mutual enrichment, tend to overlook that intergroup contacts remain limited, and the final demand is that the incoming people be ready to assimilate. Despite all the spoken good intentions, as long as the out-group remains visible (e.g., African Americans in the United States), it also remains relatively underprivileged.

Figure 2.2. Three Ways of Relating to "Others"

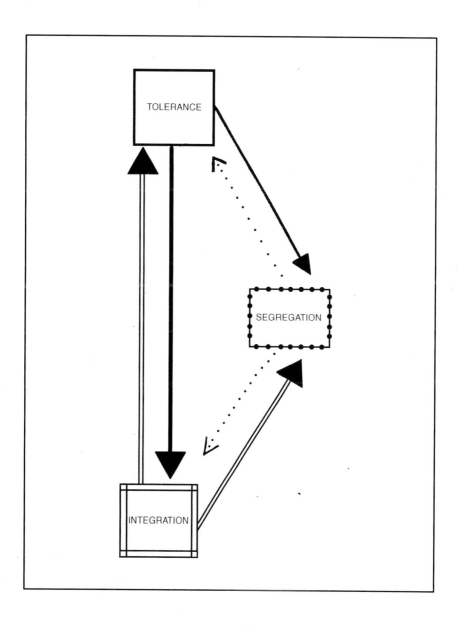

As we approach the twenty-first century, we must pioneer new pathways for seeking equality (as described in Chapter 3).

SUMMARY

This chapter began with an analysis of four causes or components of all continuing intergroup conflicts, and focused especially on the impact of asymmetric power situations on how local establishments tend to treat their weak groups. Both the segregation-domination and the integration models were examined, as were the limits of a tolerance approach. The need for something additional is emphasized.

EXERCISES

Segregation and Bigotry

What connection do you see between racism and bigotry, ignorance about others, and continuing segregation? In your experience, how might a community try to cope with or eliminate this phenomenon?

Is Integration a Long-Range Solution?

Compare the advantages and disadvantages of integration in a pluralistic modern society. Give your reasons for supporting or opposing it.

Chapter 3

Coexistence

SOME PHILOSOPHIC-HISTORICAL DEVELOPMENTS

In the history of Western societies, early developments are usually interconnected with a religious orthodoxy. According to early Judaism, Christianity, and Islam, strangers (i.e., people whose looks or behavior are not in accordance with local norms) were seen as untrustworthy, inferior, or outright sinful. Nonconformists were made to feel guilty, often subject to violent punishment, and, if left alive, enslaved. Procedures for conversion into the norms of the establishment society were very strict. Ideas such as integration or coexistence were totally outside this paradigm.

In Renaissance Europe, the rejection of strangers began to change. As part of the Enlightenment, strange languages and cultures became exotic and interesting. Thinkers began to differentiate between religious commandments and social customs. A century later, sophisticated doctors and scholars accepted Sigmund Freud's suggestion that people showing many kinds of "bizarre" behavior were perhaps psychologically sick and might be healed or rehabilitated. In contrast to the "sinful" unwed mother in Nathaniel Hawthorne's *The Scarlet Letter,* nonconformists no longer deserved to be punished and humiliated.

In the nineteenth century, early sociologists and anthropologists began to define deviant behaviors in objective terms, and strangers were seen as potentially either interesting or enriching.

As in Canada or the United States, floods of diverse refugees and immigrants made necessary the provision of services for people from many cultures. Gradually, efforts were made to guarantee the civil rights of such newcomers (Montville, 1989).

Both citizens of the host country and members of immigrant groups, aware that they now lived with entire neighborhoods of diverse ethnic populations, had to work hard to overcome their fears, prejudices, and stereotypes. As the self-image of Canadians and Americans became more pluralistic, a multicultural reality slowly gave birth to concepts such as "melting pot," integration, tolerance, and coexistence (Spiegel, 1997; Williams, 1997).

RECOGNIZING A NEW PARADIGM

To look at this phenomenon, we have to expand Figure 2.2 into a four-variable model (see Figure 3.1). Coexistence is usually mentioned in connection with the term "pluralism." The latter indicates that more than one kind of reality exists, or that any one reality is composed of many parallel entities. In sociological terms, coexistence means that members of diverse ethnic, racial, religious, and social groups both maintain their own traditions and autonomy and live comfortably within a common civilization. Thus, it becomes a policy of living side by side in peaceful interdependence—within the same spatial or temporal boundaries. Intergroup relations are based on equality, high participation, exchange, and mutuality. No participating group is expected to deculturate; in fact, the emphasis is on healthy levels of identity and assertiveness.

In heterogeneous or pluralist societies, the proponents of coexistence argue that it is acceptable to be different, as long as we respect one another's uniqueness and rights (within a flexible range of normative citizen behaviors). Actually, some nonconformist behavior, and a reasonable degree of uncertainty, are taken to be wholesome for a pluralist society (even so, it may be necessary to

Figure 3.1. Four Ways of Relating to "Others"

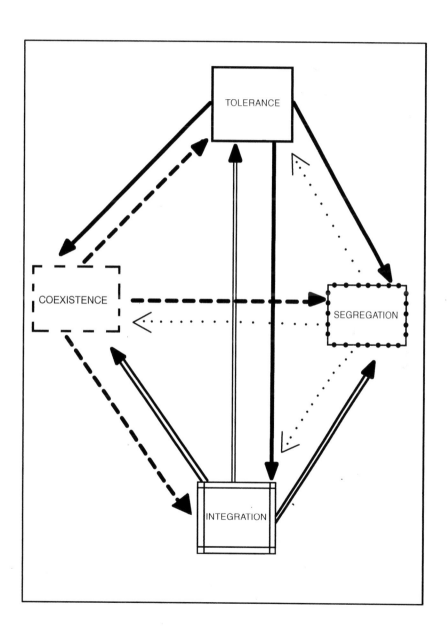

make bigotry a punishable offense). Enabling legislation could also enact a range of incentives for those who do try to live according to this new paradigm.

Scholars suggest that a coexistence society be conceptualized as a mosaic. Based on positive self-esteem, each member of such a society respects the culture, language, and so on of others with whom they have ongoing relationships. A country with such a pluralistic approach may, for example, create a policy of bi- or trilingualism, as well as sponsor programs of intergroup encounter meetings for various age cohorts.

The 1992 directory of the philanthropic Abraham Fund suggests that, in the Middle East, coexistence is the only alternative. Instead of denying the distinctiveness of various intranational, national, and international groups, the coexistence approach legitimates ethnic differences and other forms of diversity. It makes "otherness" a reason for learning to live in an atmosphere of mutual respect. Now, identity is based on traditions that allow one to feel proud without needing to believe oneself to be better than someone else.

SOME COEXISTENCE PARAMETERS

Part of our preparation for life today must include learning skills for coping with initial uncertainty and for members of diverse social groups (with differing values, political loyalties, customs, religions, languages, historical experiences, norms of behavior, etc.) to live alongside one another peacefully. In a pluralistic society, diverse peoples are expected to "manage" together at the same time and in the same geographic space—as respected and legally equal units. Willing to risk living with others unlike themselves, they become strong enough to do so without succumbing to simplistic dichotomies or stereotypic generalizations. They also believe that individuals with multiple loyalties or identities may be trusted as neighbors and fellow citizens

(Chetkow-Yanoov, 1986; Gibb, 1978). Policy-level decision making is relatively decentralized and rises from the grassroots level. Because such a society respects diversity, being different does not make someone a stranger.

Analysis of recent developments in Northern Ireland suggests another facet of coexistence. Today, people in Ireland (and in Europe generally) are beginning to understand that peoples of marked historic and cultural differences can work together without sacrificing any of their sovereignty. The reconciliation between France and Germany after World War II is an eloquent example. As the independent nation-state ceases to be our primary focus, the norms of shared sovereignty or interdependence (i.e., of international or intercultural coexistence) are being taken more and more seriously (Hume, 1993).

For coexistence to succeed, all groups must admit their interdependence and accept responsibility for one another's basic survival. Intergroup relations are based on self-respect, respect for others, and the ability to engage in dialogue about painful or controversial topics. Cooperation generates what Ruth Benedict called "synergy"—outcomes that are greater than a sum of the separate contributions of each participant (Benedict, 1970; Harris, 1970). Groups do some things together on a basis of trust, common interests, and learning a good deal about each other, but they also work hard to retain their unique culture (see Figure 3.2).

If a society operates on the basis of shame, anxiety, fear, neglected needs, and suspicion, "others" remain not-to-be-trusted strangers (convenient for scapegoating when things do not go well). Unrestrained competition can lead to rivalry, cheating, exclusion, and hatred (as well as exploitation, victimization, economic deprivation, and racism). The weaker or minority groups will likely be enraged, and long for revenge. If the latter are dominated into submission, members of this weak population may also suffer from shame and self-hate.

Figure 3.2. Characteristics of Domination versus Coexistence

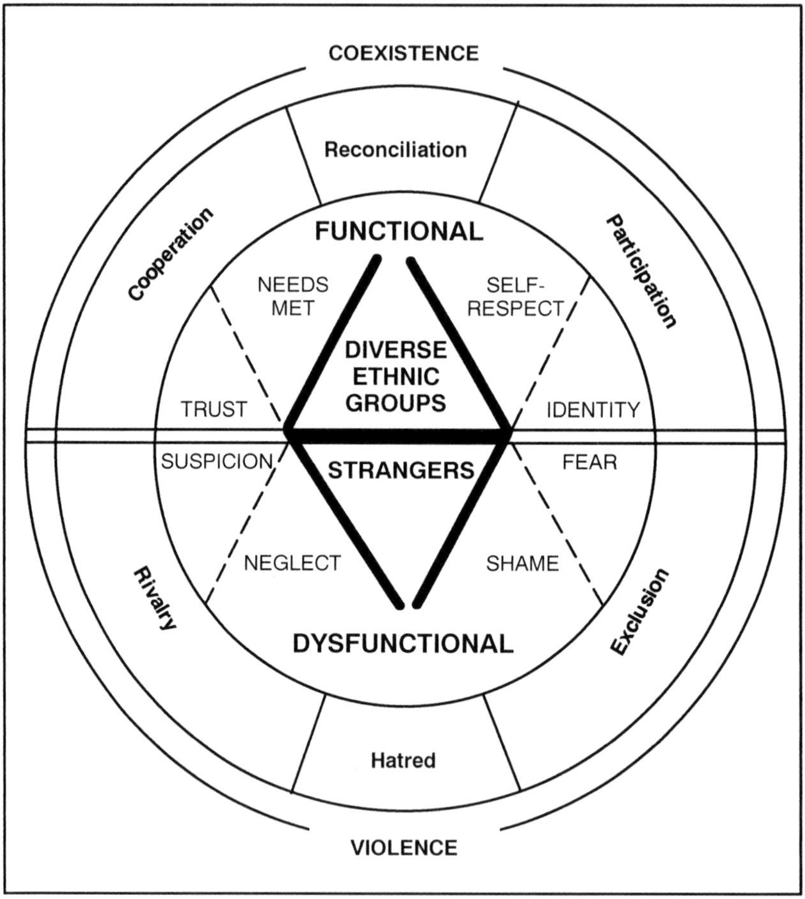

On the other hand, when a society functions according to principles such as participation, reconciliation, and cooperation—and its citizens have self-respect and a healthy identity, are able to trust others, and feel that their basic needs are being met—diversity will be seen in a favorable light. Healthy belonging and assertiveness should allow for psychological security, and provide the necessary basis for risk taking, high levels of exchange, and partnership arrangements. Such a society is likely to have traditional forgiveness techniques and ceremonies (e.g., smoking a peace pipe among Native Americans, or the *sulcha* still practiced by Druze and Bedouins in Israel). Each participant or group in a coexistence reality volunteers to give up some sovereignty in exchange for the tangible benefits that emerge from their cooperative efforts (Foa and Foa, 1980; Heath, 1976).

COEXISTENCE-PROMOTING STRUCTURES AND STRATEGIES

Since coexistence is almost synonymous with exchange and mutuality, certain social structures seem to enhance such processes and outcomes. Interdepartmental committees or councils are structured to bring participating units together on equal footing. The same is true of federations and coalitions. Many block or neighborhood clubs also operate on the principle of participation of equals. In most of these structures, people cooperate because they can be heard, and the win-win outcomes mean that they, too, benefit in some tangible way. A process of give and take (called exchange) is basic to all these structures. Obviously, bureaucratic pyramids of power and influence will produce domination, not coexistence.

In fact, certain action strategies and skills seem appropriate to the coexistence field. When the participants know how to bargain, negotiate, and compromise, the probability of cooperation is enhanced. If the other is seen as a legitimate partner (making legitimate efforts to satisfy his or her needs), and the services of a skilled mediator are available, multiple levels of cooperation prove possible (see Figure 3.3). Based on multicultural realities of Canada in the 1990s, the type of structure shown in Figure 3.3 enables the interests of many participants to overlap, and diverse arenas are created for cooperation among two, three, and all four of those involved.

Figure 3.3. A Structure for Multiple Coexistence in Canada

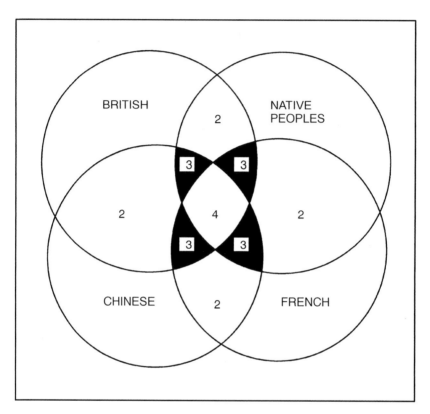

As will be elaborated in Chapter 6, coexistence can be found in many parts of the world. Members of diverse ethnic groups show potential for coexistence in Hawaii, Namibia, and Canada. In the Middle East, Israeli, Egyptian, and Jordanian environmentalists are working together in an unprecedented program for protecting the Gulf of Akaba (Maranz, 1993). Arabs and Jews are coexisting in mixed cities such as Lod and Haifa, in the municipal theater of Be'er Sheva, and in all of Israel's Tennis Center branches. A few twenty-first-century leaders are even daring to suggest that the future of Jerusalem depends on making it a place of joint sovereignty.

Three other examples should be mentioned. In the field of religion, lay and clerical participants are starting to develop a theology of pluralism or ecumenicism (Cracknell, 1994). Similar trends are seen among the publishers of children's literature (Jones, 1991). In Israel, on the way to Jerusalem, Jews and Arabs live together and operate a bilingual *moshav* called Neve Shalom (Oasis of Peace)—elaborated upon in Chapter 6. We hope that these examples become contagious.

SUMMARY

Coexistence with a mosaic of diverse neighbors is an enriching experience. Within it, decentralized decision making rises from grassroots origins. There is general agreement that the benefits make the effort worthwhile. It produces a type of society that respects difference and learns to live with a measure of unpredictability. This approach seems appropriate for a planet full of increasingly pluralistic neighborhoods, cities, and nations.

Actually, coexistence requires that all groups share power and resources—rather than letting anyone accumulate a monopoly. Unique population groups choose to cooperate with one another on matters of common interest because such behavior brings them desirable rewards (Chetkow-Yanoov, 1985). Moreover, coexistence makes for increased participation.

EXERCISES

De-Escalating Intergroup Conflicts in Different Societies

What are the chances for successfully de-escalating a conflict between rival ethnic groups in:

(a) a segregationist society?
(b) a coexistence society?

As part of your answer for either of these societies, describe an example of such a process, and suggest some reasons why it did or did not succeed.

Coexistence Can Be on the Basis of Language

How do three language-based cultures coexist successfully in Switzerland?

Why is this so difficult to achieve in Belgium?

Some Social Structures Seem to Enhance Coexistence

How do a council, coalition, interdepartmental committee, or a federation manage to enhance coexistence relationships?

Why does bureaucracy not do so?

Making Difficult Choices

Compare and contrast two basic characteristics (e.g., decision-making patterns, coping with risks or dangers, attitudes to strangers) under conditions of segregation, integration, and/or coexistence.

Chapter 4

Creating Community Readiness for Coexistence

WORKING ON OUR OWN FEELINGS

As discussed in Chapter 1, the past few hundred years of human history have been characterized by situations of powerful ruling elites that controlled various social subgroups by keeping them in a victim status. In most cases, continuing oppression of a dependent social group leads to patterns of rebellion, terrorism, and establishment counterviolence (for example, in such countries in the twentieth century as Algeria, Egypt, [Nazi] Germany, India, Israel, Ireland, Lebanon, Nigeria, Rwanda, Spain, or Yugoslavia).

Figure 4.1 suggests that a transition from a negative interdependence to a positive one is possible—if certain remedial actions can be undertaken. For example, if both victimizers and victims undergo a basic kind of healing, their catharsis will include repentance by the one and forgiveness by the other. Practitioners of process-oriented psychology do such healing between large groups of people in deep conflict (Mindell, 1995). A successful healing experience usually produces a parallel effort to learn some objective information about the other side and enhances mutual trust.

Figure 4.1. From Oppression to Partnership

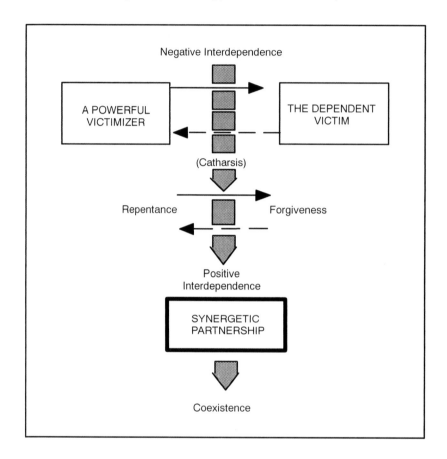

As former negative interdependence turns into limited types of partnership, tentative coexistence behaviors can begin to replace the enmity of former years. If the new experience proves to be pragmatically worthwhile, both sides find incentives to continue, and their working together creates a new kind of mutually beneficial synergy. People who emerge from former victimhood into true freedom will be able to engage in social action together.

THE IDEA OF SOCIAL ACTION

Community-level intervention has been part of social work for more than fifty years (Pray, 1947). Such issues as continuing poverty, racism, sexism, urban decay, bureaucratization, street violence, neighborhood neglect, child pornography, and drug and alcohol abuse have caused concern for years, and continue to do so all over the world. Lately, these have been supplemented by concern about the spread of intergroup conflict, increasing environmental pollution, cuts in the budgets of many social services (in the interest of deficit reduction), and the privatization of many formerly governmental services. More and more people are concluding that—as much as individuals and families continue to require therapeutic and supportive assistance—our entire societal system also requires changing or transforming.

Social workers continue to operate with individuals (micro- or casework practice) and therapeutic or task-oriented groups (mezzo-practice). In addition, more efforts are being devoted to bringing about change at organizational, neighborhood, and communitywide levels (macropractice). After benign neglect for most of this century, awareness is growing that often, in order to reduce the misery of large population groups, community social workers have to intervene with local and regional leaders, politicians, bureaucrats, and policymakers (Netting, 1993; Ross and Lappin, 1967). In other words, macropractice social workers are expected to engage in responsible social action. The community work approach is equally applicable to promoting coexistence in today's world (Chetkow-Yanoov, 1984; Chin and Benne, 1969).

This activist practice of social work requires a very assertive stance. Its practitioners are expected to foster processes of citizen participation, to enable multiorganizational coordination and planning, as well as to function effectively with various policymakers and wielders of power (Alinsky, 1946; Cox and Garvin, 1970;

Snow, 1960). Rothman (1970) summarizes the topic by proposing three basic types of community work: community development, social planning, and social action (see Table 4.1).

TABLE 4.1. Rothman's Three Models of Macropractice

	Community Development	Social Planning	Social Action
Assumptions	Community bonds disintegrating; apathy	Community suffering from social problems; e.g., poverty, child abuse, crime	Community victimized by structured inequalities
Social Work Values	Dignity of the individual; a humane social environment	Dignity of the individual; a humane social environment	Dignity of the individual; a humane social environment
Goals	Community integration and participation	Policy and program development in specialized fields	Redistribution of resources; structural change
Strategies	Encouraging citizen participation among a wide cross-section of community interests	Convincing policymakers to adopt improved social policies and social programs	Organizing victimized groups to challenge unjust structures
Tactics	Cooperation to promote organization and consensus among institutions and community groups; conflict to remove obstacles to strengthening community bonds	Cooperation with power holders within state bureaucracies to gain credibility for proposed reforms; conflict to remove obstacles to reforms	Cooperation with victimized groups to promote political consciousness and organization; conflict with elite power groups
Examples	Neighborhood and self-help groups; interagency committees; citizen councils	Government planning units; social development councils	Human rights, labor, feminist, and peace movements

Rothman's analysis, although considered a bit old-fashioned today, is a useful way to make a first acquaintance with the field. The three macropractice foci, like three intersecting circles, can be observed to have some activities in common (in the areas of overlap). They need not be seen as sequential, but they sometimes help explain phases of a specific episode of community action. Metaphorically, they can be visualized as the roots (community development), stem (social planning), and flowers (social action) of a growing plant (Rothman, 1970, 1974; Rothman, Erlich, and Tropman, 1995).

Some contemporary scholars are unhappy with this trilogy. They see community work as a product of directive and nondirective energies—including task or process goals, initiatory and enabling roles, or instrumental (how to get things done) versus expressive (how to express feelings) functioning (York, 1984). Others analyze macropractice efforts in terms of the tactics used by its practitioners—collaborative, competitive, or adversarial (Netting, Kettner, and McMurty, 1993). Zander (1990) adds an insightful description of the various ways macrochange agents use social pressure to force targeted groups or organizations to change and/or to engage in systemwide reform.

As is obvious in Table 4.2, my analysis focuses on four overlapping types of community practice: development, competition, planning, and reform.

Development

Conditions of self-choice of both goals and means are conducive to community development. Ideally, decisions that are the product of consensus lead to successful self-help (as when the parents of handicapped children organize themselves into a voluntary service association). Cultural norms are respected, especially regarding the

TABLE 4.2. A Four-Component Model of Macropractice

Types of Means Used	How Project Goals Are Chosen	
	Flexibly and Inclusively	**Closedly and Exclusively**
Nondirective and Participatory	1. DEVELOPMENT Self-help of equals Process and consensus Guide facilitates e.g., block club	3. PLANNING Reluctant collaboration Compromise pragmatically Mediator enables e.g., urban renewal
Directive and Risky	2. COMPETITION Normative rivalry Look for own gain Expert consults e.g., coalition	4. REFORM Predetermined goals Partisan use of power Activist implements e.g., lobbying

choice of means to be used. The process of development is based on listening to grassroots expressions of needs and wants, and on widespread involvement of all relevant participants. If professional persons are involved, their role is very nondirective, such as the facilitator/guide who brings a group of tourists to the place in which they expressed interest.

Competition

In politics and commercial sports, the parties confront each other and make strenuous efforts to win. Such groups often seek the directive help of an expert consultant or a coach. For example, members of a labor union may protest against (i.e., compete for power with) the management of their workplace by means of boycotts, mass rallies, public embarrassment, or outright strikes.

Members of an existing group or organization may, when feeling secure, be willing to rise above their former rivalry and choose to cooperate with others having similar interests—especially if everybody benefits from such a joint effort. Political party coalitions, a council of regional churches, or a forum of neighborhood committees exemplify this phenomenon.

Planning

When, for example, competing organizations have contrasting suggestions for the utilization of a downtown property, their claims usually come before the municipal zoning board or the regional planning commission. Even if they believe that these public service bureaucracies are being arbitrary, the competitors may agree to compromise on principles so that the service's benefits are not lost (Brager and Jarrin, 1969). Under opportune conditions (such as potential large-scale profits), members of different partisan groups may decide to share or exchange resources on a short-term basis. If the desires of all parties are not taken into account, the community may well suffer continuing competition. This can paralyze a community or lead to reform (such as the one initiated by Reverend Martin Luther King Jr.). If a settlement is reached, it is often the product of expert mediation or arbitration (Rubin, 1985).

Reform

Serious active change is usually the result of both goals and means being chosen deliberately. A partisan action group (e.g., that of Ralph Nader in the United States) does not compete with the local establishment. In using power in sophisticated ways to bring about widespread change (according to its goals), it may well indulge in lobbying or resort to semimanipulative actions. Military intervention does this to the losers. However, when a group of radically inspired influential people (in the United

States) decided to innovate what is now the Social Security system, many others benefited from this change. The same conditions apply to short-term disaster relief services after a serious flood or earthquake. Such a serious effort, as when an alcoholic undergoes therapy, may go beyond mere change; that is, the relevant system may become transformed.

Those who engage in social action to cause a society to move toward coexistence (a form of transformation) are likely to use the means and tactics of reform. The rest of this chapter suggests various ways to use social action for promoting and strengthening a coexistence policy at community and/or national levels.

TWO WAYS FOR CITIZENS TO TAKE ACTION

Citizens who are deeply dissatisfied with the way things are going have a number of options for taking action. Two of them are described in this section.

Becoming a Politician

In a democratic society, a concerned citizen (especially if backed by money and a political party) may campaign for a political office and get elected. Not everyone is interested in wielding political power, but those who (as grassroots precinct workers, or as elected members of a city council or a legislature) find politics stimulating may be able to change existing legislation, propose a new law, or bring about an increase in budget allocation for important projects.

In the case of promoting multiculturalism in Canada in 1975, the clear backing of then–Prime Minister Trudeau rapidly moved this policy into the implementation stage (Draft Report, 1975). A policy change is even more probable if the sponsor follows it through the legislative process and/or is willing to horse-trade with other politicians pushing their pet projects.

To enjoy a political life, the practitioner is likely to subscribe to values that many citizens either support or oppose. Today, politicians (along with leaders of local establishments) in countries all over the world seem prepared to reduce the budgets of welfare, health, and education services, to punish those who are poor or dependent, or to insist that services become more efficient by downsizing (Chetkow-Yanoov and Nadler, 1978). In the last years of the twentieth century, when many conservative governments have been elected, someone committed to serving poor or dependent human beings, expanding social agency services, or promoting an independent authority for coexistence is not likely to feel comfortable in politics. Such a person will probably do well to find nonpolitical ways to engage in social reform.

Engaging in Organized Protest

As in Korea and Serbia during January 1997, citizen groups can be rallied into protests against an undesirable policy. Massive numbers, acting in a disciplined manner, are sometimes able to get the establishment to discontinue a coercive or manipulative activity. Such efforts include nonviolent rallies, disruption of services, causing a work slowdown, boycott or strike, resigning, or stimulating an embarrassing exposé in the media (Hardcastle, Wencour, and Powers, 1997; Moran, 1992; Specht, 1969). The protests under Mahatma Gandhi's leadership were a necessary prelude to ending the British rule of India.

We would do well to remember that no matter how effective a protest may be, the Bible states that ceasing to do evil is not enough. To bring about significant change, we are admonished also to do good and to pursue the desired goal actively (Psalm 34:15). Organized protest may indeed get everyone to notice and reject an ongoing evil, but this phase should be followed by ideas for solving the underlying problem, and then by implementing a feasible alternative plan (see discussion of lobbying).

All these are relevant to creating a grassroots as well as community-wide desire for a policy of coexistence, and for getting such a policy implemented (Lipsky, 1968).

PROFESSIONAL WAYS TO TAKE ACTION

Some forms of community action are more likely to succeed if they include the efforts of sophisticated macropractice professionals. The three types of deliberate action described in this section all aim to influence key authorities and decision makers while staying within local norms (e.g., not resorting to violence). The challenge is to make sophisticated use of existing social, democratic, political, and legal structures to get unacceptable current conditions improved.

Empowering Citizens to Take Action

One way to engage in deliberate social change is to empower weak citizen groups or organizations, so that they find the courage to demand long-denied rights and learn the skills for exerting social pressure effectively (Kornblum and Liebman, 1975). Training sessions and role-play exercises help grassroots citizens learn how to cohere together, how to know their opponent (or oppressor), how to get around bureaucratic rigidities, and how to utilize the courts (Chetkow, 1968). Neighborhood association members who attend city council meetings regularly, and know (for example) how to make a show of taking notes silently, should be able to get the politicians' attention, bring an end to the neglect of their interests, and start a process of change.

Citizen groups can also be taught how to exert pressure by means of volunteering in key community settings. If, for example, retirees wish to have the inadequacy of their pensions recognized, they might offer their help (as volunteers) at police stations, public schools, television and radio stations, politicians' offices, or the chamber of commerce—and engage their hosts in focused informal "conversations." The latter may well counter the isolation of older people, as well as create activities different groups can share—thus leading toward coexistence. With the right kinds of professional help, citizens can strengthen their sense of self-respect and assertiveness—becoming able to establish self-help groups and make the rounds of local financing sources for a startup budget.

In this form of social action, macropractice professionals may engage in such roles as guide/facilitator, enabler/mediator, expert/ consultant, or implementor. They might also engage in building social networks among activist citizen groups (Hardcastle, Wencour, and Powers, 1997).

Advocacy on Behalf of the Powerless

When citizen groups (e.g., members of a long-victimized minority neighborhood) are too weak or disheartened, some powerful politician, religious leader, or macropractice professional may choose to engage in advocacy on their behalf—until they mature enough to represent their interests themselves (Brager, 1968; Sosin and Caulum, 1983). Such an advocate may challenge the status quo in a court of law, spearhead some new legislation (perhaps to put restraints on expressions of bigotry), activate existing law enforcement agencies (e.g., an ombudsman or a review board), use publicity and sensation to embarrass inactive authorities, use confrontation mechanisms (e.g., a well-publicized debate), provide expert testimony, organize a coalition of like-minded organizations, or generate and push a petition.

Advocate planners, for example, are expected to represent not only the interests of the client who engages their services but also the needs and desires of the downtrodden, the government, diverse relevant community groups, and the environment. Advocate planners are trained to cope with political opposition as well as the resistance of special-interest groups. Ideally, they take into account the impact their recommendations might have on the future of the entire community.

If they are in favor of interreligious or interethnic pluralism, and want diverse groups to move toward coexistence, professional macropractice workers will struggle (normatively) to awaken unconcerned colleagues or to challenge hostile authorities to put an item on their agendas. Advocacy is particularly important in times of crisis, when business as usual will result in widespread suffering. Hopefully, the powerless group will learn to be more assertive in the future, but during an emergency, effective advocacy is essential.

Lobbying

Powerful community interests or macropractitioners who are in favor of some policy or action may try deliberately to persuade the authorities (e.g., legislators, budgeters, the judiciary) or entice the mass media to support their ideas. The Gray Panthers do so on issues important to the country's aged (Kleyman, 1974; Percy, 1974), as do large corporations such as IBM or Shell Oil to further their own interests. Such interest groups remain committed to their agenda, that is, are "for" rather than "against" something. They often get their way by offering attractive incentives to those who adopt a project or allocate money for its implementation. In their focus on getting results, some unscrupulous lobbyists manipulate relevant decision makers with illegal means.

Lobbyists who believe in their project gather expert information, write speeches for influential people who are ready to support their cause, seek coverage in the media, or get articles published in prestigious journals. If they want a community to move toward coexistence, they might recommend that different neighbors who live side by side for a year both receive a credit on their income tax obligations. They might also supply volunteers to teach a trial semester of lessons on coexistence at a receptive high school or university (Chetkow-Yanoov, 1986).

Reformers who resort to lobbying must first be very clear regarding the change goals they want to put into operation. They need to know their overall topic thoroughly (including the history of its evolution), the political system's process and rituals of making decisions, its current ways of allocating resources (i.e., of guaranteeing an adequate budget), and its routine practices of implementing a new thrust. The probability of success is enhanced if they avoid manipulation and all forms of violence (Kelman, 1969) and are supported by prestigious advocacy agents and/or by a diversity of lobbyists from other fields (Hayes and Mickelson, 1991; Yuhui, 1996; Zander, 1990).

IMPLICATIONS

Talented macropractice workers will be skilled in all five of the options described previously. They should also be comfortable with a range of power-based tactics—from persuasion and petitions to confrontation, using formal court procedures, or inviting the news media to do an exposé. Protest and advocacy might well be used simultaneously. In fact, the likelihood of bringing about significant policy change is heightened if lobbying is preceded by well-disciplined protest.

A serious development effort should parallel or follow any large-scale social action thrust. If an initially weak group or organization is ever to become responsible for itself and its future, its members will require opportunities to learn factual knowledge as well as intervention skills. If learning can be followed by practical experience—of taking action individually or jointly with others sharing a common interest—future prospects are enhanced. The recurring riots in Los Angeles suggest that, in extreme cases of initial deprivation and/or victimization, some healing effort might be necessary (to deal with fear, long-accumulated rage, or habits of blaming others) before community development can take place.

SUMMARY

This chapter suggests how to use macro–social action to create community readiness for coexistence. Various conceptual models of macropractice are described, as are five kinds of citizen and professional efforts. Some basic principles are reviewed—as a prelude to taking steps to make coexistence operational locally.

EXERCISES

How Might Coexistence Be Enhanced?

Make up an example of how cooperative relationships are strengthened by the use of such strategies as negotiation, compromise, or bargaining.

Using Deliberate-Change Tactics for Promoting Coexistence

Identify some of the similarities and differences between advocating for a powerless group (e.g., the impoverished urban homeless) and lobbying for policy-level changes (e.g., that allocations for public education be increased).

How might these two tactics be used to promote a coexistence style of community?

Chapter 5

Specific Efforts
for Achieving Coexistence

GOAL IMPLEMENTATION
IN A PLURALIST SOCIETY

When project goals include the desire to institute or strengthen the coexistence lifestyle, sufficient resources must be available to translate such aspirations into social realities. In a pluralist or multicultural society, efforts have to be invested so that people can learn coexistence skills, have opportunities to meet others (i.e., persons unlike themselves), and choose freely to participate.

Many projects are presented here, but they become meaningful only when some person or group decides to implement them. The coming together of intentions, resources, and skills is rare, but instances of successful outcomes can be found.

EDUCATIONAL EFFORTS
FOR COEXISTENCE

Any coexistence society will invest heavily in informal socialization and formal educational services to prepare youngsters or newcomers for a coexistence lifestyle.

Some parents are convinced that their children require a chauvinistic framework in order to start life with a strong sense of identity and belonging. Even if this is accurate, older children (and many adults) should be exposed to curricula that *help to unlearn/outgrow childish values, attitudes, and habits.* For example, lessons at various curricular levels should teach that human beings can advance their careers on a basis of self-awareness, assertiveness, and actual accomplishments—not by rejecting or downgrading others. After learning sufficient self-confidence and appropriate skills, we need not be afraid of the unknown, but see it as an interesting challenge. In the Jewish tradition, bravery was first defined as the ability to conquer a city. Later, advocating a more adult version, a Biblical text suggests that bravery had to do with disciplining one's nature. As wisdom blossomed, a third (Talmudic) idea of bravery referred to those persons who can make an enemy into a friend.

In other words, school systems all over the world should agree to *teach values and practical ethics* as part of the regular curriculum (Harris, 1988). If there is a policy to teach values (e.g., tolerance or respect for others), such teaching should be done openly and use the most sophisticated pedagogic methods available. In this connection, professionals in the social sciences and the helping professions should offer themselves as consultants to local and/or national levels of their country's public education system.

There is growing acceptance of the idea that racism is a learned behavior. If so, a good curriculum can enhance the unlearning of specific negative behaviors and help pupils learn to trust and to give respect.

All schools will be expected to teach every child some aspects (e.g., history, folklore, holidays) of at least *two ethnic groups or cultures other than their own.* It is becoming fashionable to hold a conference on diversity or to do issue-related interviewing among representatives of diverse cultures. Another recommendation is that all children learn more than one language—second languages have proved effective doorways into other cultures.

The curriculum might also include a scholarly look at (a) current examples of coexistence as it is found in Canada, Switzerland,

Hawaii, or the European Union; and (b) meeting representatives of other ethnic cultures in well-structured encounter groups, joint learning or volunteering activities, and carefully planned field trips. Well-facilitated dialogue groups might analyze why being different need not mean being inferior, and that engaging in cooperation does not necessarily indicate weakness.

Widespread efforts should be made to teach all citizens *how to use modern conflict-resolution technologies* at interpersonal and intergroup levels. Mediator roles are already being taught to retired elders, adult women and men, schoolchildren, lawyers, and social workers (Kalmakoff and Shaw, 1987; Umbreit, 1995).

In this connection, all schools should teach every child the *basic skills of empathic listening and dialoguing.* These skills, which adults should learn too, can then be used for practicing nonviolent communication (see, for example, Cornelius and Faire, 1989; Rosenberg, 1983).

Sophisticated *healing and guidance services* should be made available to all persons or groups who have been exploited and abused (i.e., have suffered victimization). Reconciliation efforts might be enhanced if everyone learned how to apologize for past wrongdoing and how to forgive the victimizer (when appropriate). Such skills are essential if people are to behave in neighborly ways toward former enemies (Charney, 1990; Danieli, 1985; Kelman, 1987; Rogers, 1965; Rouhana and Bar-Tel, 1998; Stauffer, 1987).

School-based lessons might be reinforced by parallel *participatory experiences* in special summer camps, international youth seminars, organized tours of other countries, or one-year studies in a university abroad. This type of socialization is vital for lifelong learning.

The education system should make appropriate efforts to *update the contents and experiences used to train student teachers* for their professional future—in line with the previous recommendations. If coexistence values and technologies are to be taught in a wide range of school classrooms, teachers will need to have:

- been exposed to such topics,
- examined their own value commitments, and
- become convinced that such involvements are indeed professional.

Their willingness to pioneer will be enhanced if they receive support from in-school colleagues and from their national professional associations (Holmes, 1992).

Peace values and skills are not the exclusive responsibility of educators. Teachers who want to promote coexistence can strengthen their impact if they *enlist the cooperation of parents* and parent organizations. They could also find support from such related professionals as school psychologists or social workers and in organizations such as community centers and churches.

Peacemaking knowledge, attitudes, and skills, like reading or mathematics, should be taught and reviewed several times during a person's learning career. The continuum of conflict resolution lessons might start in nursery (role-playing, arts activities, etc.), and in learning to speak and read two languages. Grade 4 pupils might be exposed to peer mediation. In junior high and high school, peace-related courses might include formal academic content and be supplemented with educationally focused encounter seminars with members of another culture. Courses taught at universities might strengthen the thrust with adults and could be supplemented by continuing education programs for retirees.

COMMUNITY-WIDE EFFORTS FOR COEXISTENCE

In addition to the educational efforts previously recommended, a number of other societal factors can help promote coexistence as a way of life. One such factor is to make wide use of *positive incen-*

tives, to reward individuals and groups who agree to practice co-existence as part of their lives. In Israel, for example, Arab and Jewish citizens who have coexisted with neighbors unlike themselves for more than twelve months might both qualify for a rebate on the income tax they pay during the next year (Chetkow-Yanoov, 1984; Kettner, Dunlap, and Nichols, 1985; Rothman, 1970).

Similarly, to guarantee a basis for coexistence in a democratic society, *bigotry and victimization must become legally punishable offenses.* Real democracy goes beyond implementing the will of the majority of the voters. It should also guarantee the rights of all citizens (Alinsky, 1946). Everyone needs to grow up expecting that antidiscrimination laws are enforced objectively.

As outlined in Chapter 3, another way to promote coexistence is to support *organizational structures that enhance cooperation and coordination.* This thrust might include learning some of the basics of exchange theory (Foa and Foa, 1980), and making wider use of organizational charts that are circular rather than pyramidic (Dluhy, 1990; McCann and Gray, 1986). In nonpyramidic organizations, executive directors are transformed into coordinators.

Widespread efforts must be made to:

1. Enhance coexistence and intergroup understanding by *the mass media* and through communication technologies. Newscasts might include analysis of action options for groups currently in conflict, enable electronic intergroup contacts when great distances make personal visits too expensive, or provide a form of rapid mediation between rival parties under the guise of objective reporting (Baumann, 1993; Shepard, 1994-1995).

2. Invite *writers and performing artists* to create special programs for discovering other-culture neighbors, show a soap opera whose story focuses on intergroup understanding and cooperation, publish popular fiction and nonfiction stories (with a moral), or make a creative show on coexistence in the style of Stevie Wonder or Walt Disney.

3. Help people experience some of the *joys of diversity.* At the neighborhood level, contacts with members of another culture make possible the sampling of new foods, songs, folk dances, and holiday ceremonies. Volunteering together enhances our finding out about one another's human qualities and enables us to give informal help in an unexpected crisis. Participants at an international conference find themselves enriched by contacts with delegates from other countries and from structured encounters with their ideas (one is often excited to discover that ideas or experiences within his or her culture are confirmed by delegates from other settings). For instance, some fifty years ago, after leaders of the orthodox Jewish community of Vancouver, Canada, discovered the beauty and utility of church confirmation of Christian girls, they created a similar ceremony (the Bat Mitzvah) for their teenage girls.

4. Encourage all the helping professions to copy the example of the National Association of Social Workers—who focused one-fifth of their 1996 annual conference (in Cleveland) on the implications of *practicing social work in environments of diversity.* Helping professionals might, for example, convene special training workshops for colleagues choosing to work in the intercultural arena, or offer a prize to colleagues who publish a collection of articles on practice innovations in the diversity field.

5. Guarantee professional and legal interventions to *lessen or prevent the emergence of all forms of fanaticism.* If people's identity and sense of accomplishment are so frail that they take refuge in fundamentalism, the helping professions might try to motivate them to deal with long-lasting fears (Hoffer, 1951; Hoffman, 1982). When victims' rage is close to exploding into destructive violence, these professions might offer help with stress management to large audiences by means of radio and television.

6. Invent a variety of *symbolic reminders* for everyday use to help people become accustomed to the normality of coexistence. The following "letterhead" serves as one example (see Figure 5.1).

Figure 5.1. Symbolism in a Letterhead

Similarly, we might encourage commercial advertisers to feature both men and women, people of diverse skin colors, and speakers of many languages.

7. Give coexistence a chance; sanction a *clear separation of democracy, nationality, and religion.* In social reality, these three areas often overlap, but they are not identical. For example, in Israel orthodox Jews see no separation between religion and Jewish nationality. According to many of them, nationality and democracy must conform with the dictates of religious dogma, and there is no reason for coexisting with any other people or ideology. Some orthodox political parties feel justified in using their influence to defeat the implementation of coexistence—creating increased tension within the country.

Thus, in all societies or cultures, only a clear separation of these three functions will make coexistence probable. These concepts must themselves be able to exist side by side rather than dominate one another.

8. Encourage national nongovernmental organizations and governments to emulate the work of Australia's Conflict Resolution Network—which has made a successful effort to convince *local, state, and national politicians to become part of a conflict-resolving government* (de Haas, 1996; Suter, 1996). Politicians who joined

the campaign agreed to refrain from making personal attacks on their opponents, to discuss diverse views without abuse or denigration, to seek common ground with others, and to work toward more respectful political discussion and behavior. The CRN also developed a conflict-resolution toolkit for government.

THREE ESSENTIAL PROCESSES

The achievement of coexistence relations among diverse ethnic, racial, gender, religious, political and other groups seems to be connected to three overlapping human processes (see Figure 5.2). Trust and confidence are basic to any relationship with people or cultures initially strange to each other, as are ongoing two-way communication and readiness for cooperative activities. Specifically:

1. *Trust* is usually an outcome of being able to give credit, take risks, and communicate empathy. Trust develops during the first years of life (Erikson, 1968; Gibb, 1978). In part, it depends on a healthy self-confidence and is essential for maintaining open two-way communications.

2. *Self-confidence* has to do with being aware of one's strengths (as well as weaknesses), a feeling of belonging in some group or culture, and a pride in the positives of one's group or tradition. It is the essence of positive identity. Confident persons feel comfortable with the possibility of other people being loyal to a variety of different groups or ideologies.

3. *Open and frequent communications* with other peoples or groups are equally crucial to achieving coexistence. The latter requires that we feel comfortable in using speech, letters, video, fax, mass media, telephones, and books, as well as symbols, words, gestures, and pictures. We may also require a proficiency in listening, handling gossip, and engaging in dialogue.

Figure 5.2. Human Processes Essential for Successful Coexistence

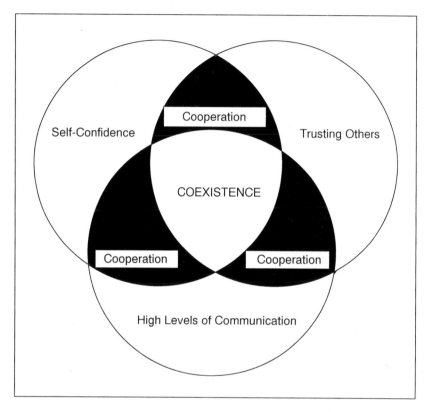

These variables enable us to cooperate with others on mutually beneficial projects. We might well be ready to participate in a council, federation, coalition, the management committee of a condominium building, a business partnership, a bulk food-buying cooperative, or the European Community.

SUMMARY

This chapter is intended for people who want to make coexistence operational in some specific geographic or ethnic setting.

Suggestions are made for implementation efforts in the education field specifically, as well as at the communitywide level. Trusting relationships, self-confidence, and open communications seem essential for the success of such change efforts.

EXERCISES

Practicing What We Preach

Suggest one political or economic thrust for helping implement the goals of coexistence in your country.

How Can I Help?

If you are a member of one of the helping professions, what ways would you suggest for promoting or enhancing trust, self-confidence, and/or open communications? Please suggest what might be done immediately, and what efforts require a long-term approach.

Chapter 6

Coexistence Efforts Around the World

THE CHALLENGE OF INNOVATING

In most human situations, as suggested in Figure 6.1, local authority and tradition preserve the status quo. Many citizens also seem to prefer a stable social environment—one in which policy and value decisions are made for them by recognized persons (e.g., kings, clan leaders) or institutions (e.g., the church, parliament). Given too much freedom to choose and/or personal responsibility, ordinary people tend to run away (Fromm, 1941). When some dissidents start to make trouble, the establishment may coopt them to keep things quiet and under control.

On the other hand, major technology changes (e.g., electricity) or new social ideas (e.g., Marxism) lead to questioning the past, a rise in discontent, and a gradual readiness to risk something new. When a conservative establishment remains rigid, it may have to face a rebellion; if it is open to change, the outcome is likely to be reform. When a change process is graced by creative leadership, the outcome may be social innovation, and can lead to progress.

The above principles apply to our progression from segregation-oppression to coexistence. In earlier historical eras, the existence of peoples, languages, or cultures different from one's own was regarded as suspicious or bad. Such people were to be expelled, conquered (enslaved, exploited), or eliminated. In stark contrast, some twentieth-century societies have undergone a paradigm shift.

Figure 6.1. Components of Change

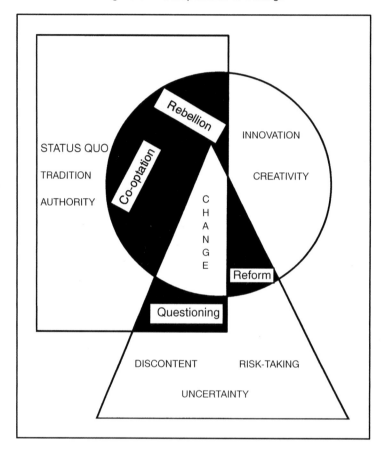

"Otherness," which once seemed evil, has been legitimized under new conceptualizations such as multiculturalism or diversity, along with the idea that dissimilar groups can coexist. It is now often fashionable to speak more than one language and to seek commonalities (or friendships) among peoples who were once defined as strangers. Contact with representatives of different ethnic groups is now seen as enriching—an essential part of modern democracy. People not only benefit from contacts with others unlike themselves, they even adapt cultural items from each other without feeling that their own identity or loyalty are compromised.

Currently, anthropologists studying diverse cultures publish in such new journals as the *European Journal of Intercultural Studies* (since 1993). The Conflict Resolution Network of Australia established a "Cultural Diversity Program" in 1991 to assist people from different cultures to communicate effectively and work together. Canada, perhaps because of its long history of bilingualism and biculturalism, established an advisory body to the Minister of State for Multiculturalism back in 1973. The Diversity Institute of the School of Social Work of Texas University at Austin is currently working to improve understanding and more effective working relationships among the unique cultures of American society. It does so by means of assessment, training, developing curriculum resources, research, policy reviews, consultations, and statewide conferences.

In this chapter, we examine a number of coexistence efforts underway in various parts of the world.

WORLDWIDE EXAMPLES OF COEXISTENCE

Canada

Canada's short history is one of a democracy struggling to find ways for French speakers, English speakers, immigrant groups, and native peoples to coexist. In such an environment of diversity, the Canadian government has taken an active role. In 1971, Prime Minister Pierre Trudeau stated, in the House of Commons, that a "policy of multiculturalism within a bilingual framework commends itself to the Government of Canada as the most suitable means of assuring the cultural freedom of Canadians." National unity was to be founded on "confidence in one's own individual identity; out of which can grow respect for that of others and a willingness to share . . ." (Draft Report, 1975). Despite continuing strains, Canada made this commitment operational in fields such as open immigration (e.g., from China, Asia, the Caribbean, all parts of Europe), public education, employment, and neighborhood development (Friesen, 1993). As the years pass and governments change, the process has slowed down, but Canada continues to exemplify the essentials of coexistence.

This characteristic is well illustrated by developments in Toronto (Cardozo, 1996). Having begun as a small town of British Protestants (with a minority of French-speaking Catholics) in the 1890s, continuing waves of immigration changed the community into a booming metropolitan area. This caused inner-city wards to become multicultural ghettoes, so that the school system began to look for ways to convert Chinese, Italian, Jewish, Greek, and other immigrant children into Canadians. In the 1960s, community-minded politicians, bureaucrats, and citizen groups worked to pass legislation protecting parks and nature areas. They also strove to encourage ethnic newspapers, create special school programs for immigrant children, and combat crime—so that Toronto became popular as "a city that works." Toronto's thrust toward equal opportunity employment is illustrated in a wall poster that reads "welcome" in many languages (part of this poster can be seen in Figure 6.2). Two education examples of Toronto-style coexistence are presented here.

Toronto Public Schools

Public education in Toronto, a three-tier (provincial-metropolitan-local) affair, has been giving sophisticated attention to the multicultural nature of the city's population for the past twenty-five years. By 1975, a massive board and staff self-study process produced a 230-page draft report that made ninety-two recommendations. The school board also allocated resources for some initial implementation steps (*We Are All Immigrants to This Place,* 1976).

Figure 6.2. Toronto's Multilingual Welcome Poster

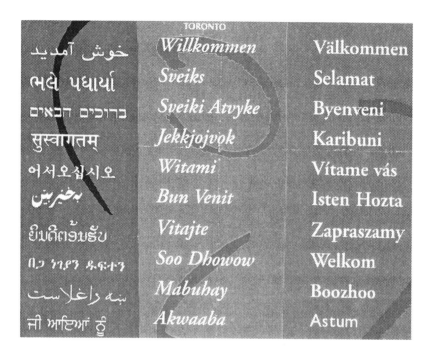

Instead of trying immediately to integrate foreign-origin children into Canadian culture, the school system teaches them English as a second language, and they may study certain topics in eighteen native tongues. A community relations staff makes energetic efforts to reach parents (in a number of languages), and parents are encouraged to become involved in local school policy and activities. School board trustees are expected to represent the diverse people of their wards when determining metropolitan education policy. Structures and group processes were set up for dealing with institutional resistance to change, as well as with incidents of racism in the school system. Training programs were designed to help teachers improve their coexistence qualifications and to be inventive in their classrooms.

In the 1980s, the school system made specific efforts to deal with the problems of black students. Racist biases were removed from textbooks. The teaching of heritage languages was instituted, especially in inner-city neighborhoods. Hiring and promotion policies were appropriately updated. A pamphlet titled *Taking Responsibility for Improving Schools* (Davies, 1995) sums it all up—teachers and parents are to be involved and consulted, the workplace is to be free of harassment, library and other support services are to be prepared and implementation is to be according to timetables and subject to a review process. In a multicultural environment, the approach is to be inclusive, and new initiatives are welcome.

The University of Toronto School of Social Work

Various studies and reports indicate that North American universities in general, and specific professions such as social work, show ignorance, insensitivity, and naivete regarding interethnic issues bordering on racism (Dominelli, 1988; McMahon and Allen-Neares, 1992; Wade, 1993). Exclusiveness seems to be put into operation by employing small numbers of minority-member administrators and teachers, by admitting few minority students, and by the monocultural curriculum focus at many institutions of higher learning. Few community leaders seem aware, or ready to admit, that neighborhood linguistic diversity in fact heralds a change from ethnic homogeneity to multiculturalism in entire urban regions.

The Toronto picture is more optimistic. In 1992, a social work initiative gave birth to a new university service called Antiracism, Multiculturalism, and Native Issues—or AMNI. The organization insisted that the University of Toronto go beyond tokenism in matters of student recruitment, faculty employment, curriculum offerings, and research undertaken. Diversity studies, which became popular, included native people (or First Nation) issues. They also focused on developing cultural competence in the delivery of social services.

During the first semester of the 1995 MSW (Master of Social Work) studies, appropriate curriculum modules were integrated into existing courses (e.g., history of welfare, research, elements of practice method, social work with immigrants, and field practice). In October 1996, after the 1995 pioneering experience, on orientation day, all first-year students were divided into small groups that were to interview citizens and officials about diversity issues. Diversity was interpreted broadly to include issues such as racism, colonialism, sexism, ageism, or harassment at work, as they exist in Toronto.

With the help of a faculty advisor, members of each group were to choose among themselves the issue, situation, or population upon which to focus. Emphasis was not on doing library research but rather on efforts to get data from interviews and personal experiences. Students were encouraged to integrate information from four of their courses, and to include their own group process, when reporting their findings to panels of faculty after a few weeks. Of course, the final oral report was to suggest some implications for the social work profession.

While on sabbatical at the Toronto School of Social Work, I advised a student group that chose to study a political ward which included long-timer, middle-class, new immigrant, and lower-class residents. Data were gathered from residents, service providers (including the police), and elected politicians. They reported on socio-economic as well as ethnic diversities in the ward, told personal stories, role-played an imaginary town meeting, and advocated a number of policy improvements. Besides documenting their own learning experiences, the students analyzed some implications for their careers as future social workers.

Holland

Holland has been a multicultural and multireligious society for hundreds of years. Although the predominant focus is Protestant and Dutch, Holland still allows for differences of religion, ethnic subcultures (e.g., of migrants or refugees from Turkey, Morocco, and Surinam), and regional dialects. In the big cities, where large non-Dutch populations have settled, some groups have started their own schools, and all are encouraged to preserve their own cultural identity (e.g., in matters of religious ceremonies, funeral practices, language spoken at home, or food and dress customs). All citizens are considered equal in the eyes of the law and are to be treated equally when seeking employment. Efforts are also being made not to let processes such as modernization and globalization homogenize Dutch culture.

In recent years, Holland continues to be a pluralist country (Couwenberg, 1997). Preserving the continuity of family-group traditions is seen as compatible with becoming acculturated into modern Holland. In schools serving multicultural neighborhoods, efforts are made to teach history objectively, all countries of origin are respected, and pupils are taught skills for coping with social difference. These schools might also employ a multicultural teaching staff. Two examples of Dutch coexistence follow.

The Multimedia Gang

The Youngsters, Education, Media (YEM) Foundation works to encourage the use of national and international press, radio, television, and digital communication networks—now considered essential for solving modern social problems. The Foundation lobbies to ensure that media education becomes available to youngsters in all countries of the European Union (Poort-van Eeden, 1997).

One of their projects is the Multimedia Gang. In this activity, Dutch children from several schools in a region cooperate with foreign youngsters living in local refugee centers. As families from diverse nationalities wait to hear whether they may stay in Holland or will be sent back to their countries of origin, groups of Dutch children visit the center, talk with their peers, and interview parents about topics such as racism. Their experiences are expressed in role-plays, reported in newspapers (and on the Internet), and made into radio and video programs that are broadcast locally.

Besides providing interesting learning opportunities for young people, this project promotes coexistence by creating opportunities for Dutch and refugee youngsters to meet other children of their age groups and to discuss topics of mutual interest. Refugee children become exposed to issues in contemporary Dutch life, while Dutch children become comfortable working with peers from other cultures. Refugee youngsters also learn how to cooperate not only with their Dutch peers but also with other-culture youngsters in their centers. All the participants learn to use modern communication media and to evaluate the effectiveness of their efforts. The skills they gain should serve them well in the future.

Multilingualism in Frisia

Unlike Belgium, where the language is officially monolingual, the Dutch province of Frisia is officially bilingual, and 500,000 residents speak Frisian at home. In 1986, after years of agitation and lobbying, Frisians succeeded in getting all their official governmental, school, and court documents published in both Dutch and Frisian.

Dutch is spoken throughout the province, but Frisians do not want to lose their identity, and they see their language as an important part of that identity. Learning Frisian is no longer forbidden—in fact, it is obligatory in the primary schools, and the language is used in lower-grade classrooms. Many of the province's municipalities use Frisian in their official documents.

Israel

Although claims of the homogeneous nature of the Jewish people can still be heard, most scholars describe world Jewry generally, and the Jews of Israel in particular, as living in clashing multi-ethnic and multicultural realities. In Israel, tensions persist between Jews of Western (Ashkenazi) and Eastern (Sephardi) origins, people of right or left political orientations, secular and religiously orthodox Jews, white and black-skinned Jews, and so on. Their lives also interlock awkwardly with those of Israeli and Palestinian Arabs, with adherents of two additional world religions, and with speakers of perhaps seventy diverse languages.

During the fifty years of modern Israel's existence, and especially after the massive immigrations of the 1950s, many action plans were tried. At first the Jews basked in a feeling of homogeneity, then newcomers were segregated into distant towns, and later efforts were made to pressure-cook everyone into an "integrated" new nationalism. The fragility of intergroup relations persisted—creating tensions and social inequalities among the Jews and between them and their non-Jewish fellow citizens. In the Middle East of the 1990s, there is an urgent need for everyone to learn some coexistence skills (Kronish, 1997; Peres and Shemer, 1984; Samooha, 1984).

Some nonconformist Israelis have experimented with components of coexistence during the past twenty years. Partnership is one voluntary organization whose members made considerable effort to learn and practice Arab-Jewish coexistence during the 1970s and 1980s (Chetkow-Yanoov, 1997). It continues this effort, on a neighborhood basis, in Haifa. Philanthropic foundations, such as the Abraham Fund, continue to support many coexistence projects and activities in Israel today (*Abraham Fund Quarterly Report,* 1997).

Neve Shalom/Wahat Al-Salam/Oasis of Peace

This hilltop cooperative village *(moshav)* in the Latrun region between Tel Aviv and Jerusalem serves as a model for Arab-Jewish coexistence. It was founded in 1972 by a visionary Catholic priest, Father Bruno, who believed that the country's two peoples and its three religions had enough common values for their members to develop a community together. The first permanent settlers arrived in 1978 and 1979, as part of a private grassroots initiative. After some harsh years of pioneering, they chose to dedicate themselves to modeling and promoting peace—with co-workers, with neighbors, and within one's self. All this evolved into a member-owned and democratically run independent small community.

By 1982, seven families (about thirty Jews and Arabs) were living in the the *moshav*. They started a joint School for Peace that operates Arab-Jewish encounter groups, trains teachers and group leaders, gives consultation on the making of peace curricula, and holds workshops for groups who request them. Gradually they became binational, bicultural, and bilingual. By 1985, they had reached 5,000 Jewish and Arab schoolchildren, trained many teachers and student teachers, and conducted workshop weekends to promote understanding and cooperation between Israeli Jews and Arabs (*Neve Shalom Newsletter*, September, 1996).

By 1992, the community had developed a series of summer evening adult education lectures, given by university scholars and Knesset (Israeli Parliament) members. The community became a partner for training Tel Aviv University psychology students in the management of intercultural encounter groups. The mayor of Tel Aviv, Shlomo Lahat, visited Neve Shalom, and was full of praise for the work they were doing. To further promote peace, the community started a commercial guest house. Its opening ceremony was attended by ambassadors of twelve countries (*Neve Shalom Newsletter*, May-August, 1992).

In 1993, after overcoming considerable political resistance, the community's nursery, kindergarten, and primary school were recognized by the regional council of the Ministry of Education. The schools began attracting children from neighboring Arab and Jewish communities. Special efforts were necessary to attract more

Jewish pupils, so that the school could function in a truly bicultural and bilingual manner. Visitors became familiar—including representatives from other countries (such as Britain, Egypt, Holland, Germany, Italy, Japan, and Switzerland) and various Israeli teacher seminaries. As one of the community residents said, "We are no longer only a symbol."

By 1995, some 150 Jewish and Arab families were on a list of applicants wanting to live at Neve Shalom. More classrooms were added, since the local school now taught ninety pupils. A tourism office began attracting study-vacation groups. Despite the financial crisis of rapid growth, the education program expanded to encompass a joint project with the YMCA and the Adam Institute of Jerusalem, one-national and binational educational projects, an academic course with Ben Gurion and Tel Aviv universities, training consultations, week-long summer courses, and an exchange program with children from Germany. A course for Arab and Jewish women and courses for Palestinian schools were developed (*Neve Shalom Newsletter,* November, 1995).

By 1996, Neve Shalom had an Internet site and was offering a list of publications to interested purchasers. The community also started a project for Arab and Jewish senior citizens in Jaffa. Community delegations were sent to Holland, Italy, Norway, and the United States, as well as to a UNESCO conference in Jordan.

As its waiting list of applicants continued to grow, Neve Shalom tried to purchase land for expansion, but encountered both regional and national governmental opposition (which it is challenging in court). The *moshav* is now deeply committed to a program of public education regarding its binational (Arab-Jewish) focus and enlisting public support for its need to expand, as well as taking the necessary legal steps. By becoming a larger community, it hopes to be able to raise the quality of life and services for its residents as well as to be taken seriously by the people of Israel (*Neve Shalom Newsletter,* January, 1998).

The January *Neve Shalom Newsletter* tells of two other developments. In June and July 1997, Neve Shalom served as the site for a three-day meeting of Jordanian, Palestinian, and Israeli governmental delegates and some experts from the European Union, negotiating the distribution of regional water resources. The *moshav* also hosted an ice-breaking workshop for American, Israeli, and Palestinian representatives in Israel to set up bilingual programs for the TV show *Sesame Street.* After filming began, Neve Shalom children were recruited to act in some of the programs.

Namibia

The history of Namibia goes back to prehistoric times, when it was peopled by hunter-gatherer cultures. Being relatively remote from Europe, it did not enter into Western history until Portuguese explorers reached its shores in the fifteenth century. It was subsequently of interest to the Dutch East India Co., to British whalers, and to English missionaries early in the nineteenth century. It was annexed by Germany in 1884, as part of its industrial revolution needs, and transferred to Britain by the League of Nations after Germany lost World War I. The British passed this mandated territory to South African jurisdiction in 1920. After almost 100 years of German colonialism and South African apartheid, and after thirty years of armed struggle against South African rule, Namibia became an independent country on March 21, 1990.

During the later years of violent armed struggle, three parallel developments made this achievement unique. First, efforts toward independence were paralleled by considerable international support, at the United Nations and in the region, to persuade South Africa to end its occupation and exploitation of the country. Chester Crocker, U.S. Assistant Secretary of State for Africa, played a key role in this process during the 1980s. Second, the Namibian guerrillas and politicians were committed to a program of interethnic reconciliation (i.e., they never accepted apartheid) many years before achieving independence, and implemented it successfully after independence. Third, during the crucial few years before independence, black and white Namibian leaders were able to meet, design a constitution, prepare for a national assembly, and set up basic guarantees of human rights and free speech. Over 90 percent of those eligible turned out for, and voted in, the country's first elections (Forrest, 1994; Sparks and Green, 1992).

During the first two years of independence, a bicameral government was set up, governmental powers were separated, the country was redivided into thirteen regions, and many local governments were elected. Private media were established, Afrikaans and German radio stations began to broadcast, white cultural clubs were allowed to continue, and an independent judicial system started functioning. Significantly, the principle of national reconciliation continued, so that, for example, revenge activities against whites did not take place, former colonial governmental employees continued to function, and steps were taken to guarantee a high-standard civil service. Attention was focused on respected roles for traditional chiefs and headmen, on maintaining urban infrastructures and services, on the needs of the impoverished and landless rural poor, on the advisability of forming additional parties, on expanding the private sector, and on the need for the country to become economically self-reliant. Interestingly, Namibians speak English, German, and nine native languages (Jabri, 1990; Nathan, 1992).

The contrast with postapartheid South Africa is clear (Friedman, 1997). Namibia came into being without a need to exploit scapegoats or blame others. Former underdogs had no need to get even or take over political power by force. White and black elites knew and respected each other enough to cooperate in setting up and running their country together. "The Namibian experience provides evidence that such an approach can work in a fractured and war-riven country moving away from all the problems of apartheid" (Simon, 1993, p. 73). Traditions of tolerance (for example, from earlier Bushman culture) and an open political culture have produced a struggling coexistence society that is probably unique in the third world.

United States

The 4-H Program

In 1914, the U.S. Department of Agriculture gave birth to a grassroots program for rural youth. Calling it the 4-H (Head-Heart-Hands-Health) Program, members of these afterschool clubs were expected to learn and use new home economics and agricultural practices. As a result of social changes in the United States, today half of all 4-H participants live in towns and cities, and almost 30 percent are members of racial or ethnic minorities. Not surprisingly, the 4-H movement began addressing multiculturalism issues in the past decade (Hofer, 1997).

Programs have been developed to help young people examine stereotypes and cultural symbols. Children learn to look at similarities and differences based on personality traits and patterns of identity, rather than on skin color or ethnicity. In addition to learning about nutrition, insects, or composting, kids prepare for adulthood by learning to appreciate diversity and to work together in multicultural teams. Activities may include genealogy studies, shared space games, human treasure hunts, or describing the ethnic characteristics of the Purple People from Plum Planet.

In certain schools, the 4-H Program tackles prejudice by devising ways for the children to deal with playground grievances and aggressions. Nationally and locally, the organization is reaching out to unserved or high-risk populations. Hofer also describes an Asian-American community in which children from ten different ethnic groups work together in gardening and community clean-up projects. These efforts include reaching out to children of

Native American tribes—with programs of training for the students and teachers of local schools who want to cope with the challenges of cultural diversity.

Coexistence Programs at Brandeis University

With the resources of two special endowment funds, Brandeis University is bringing Israeli Jews and Israeli Arabs to campus for four years of study. These students are exposed to programs promoting empathy and understanding. After they meet, the young people seek out areas of common interest in one another's everyday lives. Over a period of time, as they become friends, they find themselves able to discuss very sensitive or charged issues and to engage in joint dialogue. They meet socially in various classes as well as have opportunities to study one another's culture, traditions, and history together. Daily encounters, improved communication skills, and joint service activities help them to identify areas of common interest and to respect one another's heritage.

Back in Israel during the summers and after completing their studies, they make trips together and visit one another's homes. Their parents are encouraged to meet and to engage in adult activities together. As the young people and the adults accumulate accurate knowledge about one another and share joint experiences, they become ready to take risks and become more prepared to coexist peacefully (Lyon, 1997).

Another program at Brandeis University focuses specifically on coexistence fellowships. Based in the International Center for Ethics, Justice, and Public Life, this new program encourages participants from diverse backgrounds to undertake a process of learning what coexistence means and to develop ways for historically divided peoples to live and work together within societies that have become multicultural. The Center intends to aid scholars and practitioners worldwide to wrestle with the complex relationship between these coexistence projects and the many long-standing issues of social, political, and economic justice in their home countries.

Participants are expected to engage in discussions, seminars, workshops, artistic presentations, and lectures designed to improve their capacity to reflect upon, design, and implement coexistence projects. They are to learn theory, refine their conflict resolution skills, share narratives about their lives and work, and explore relevant complex ethical dilemmas. Funds are available to support coexistence projects within the students' home countries, as well as internationally.

IMPLICATIONS

Many things must be done, and soon, to prepare diverse world populations and subgroups for living in a reality of ethnic-cultural pluralism. After experiencing processes of healing (to help us get over past wounds and humiliations), we may all have to go through a major paradigm shift.

With the help of parents, peers, and childhood educators, we must learn how to form our identity in positive ways that do not require us to be better than some other group. Although they sometimes overlap, we have to learn how to separate identities based on nationalism (e.g., Israeli or Palestinian or Irish) from those based on religion (Judaism or Islam or Catholicism). In fact, to eliminate dangerous anxieties and ignorance, educational curricula of the twenty-first century will have to include organized contacts with ethnic groups and indigenous cultures other than our own, so that we can stop equating differentness with inferiority. We will want opportunities to learn values and skills that enable us to solve problems and coexist as partners—rather than to fear, blame each other, or oppress those who choose not to assimilate into our society. Today, it has become crucial that we learn the dynamics of dialogue and sharing, and cease debates or giving status to those who win a competition.

These suggestions must also be backed by political leaders and government bureaucrats. Reaching a coexistence reality has to be the product of policy, legislation, and law enforcement as well as childhood socialization. Of course, coexistence could be enhanced by a functional system of conflict resolution and an attractive range of incentives. In a coexistence society, resolving conflicts and creating new partnerships should be encouraged among diverse religions, age groups, the sexes, business and ecology interests, language groups, political parties, and military factions, as well as ethnic cultures. Today we have evidence that it is cheaper to share power than to fight over it.

SUMMARY

This chapter makes operational the paradigm shift that has been discussed and analyzed earlier in the book. It describes successful examples of coexistence in such diverse parts of the world as Canada and the United States (North America), Holland (Europe), Israel (the Middle East), and Namibia (southwestern Africa). In places where a participatory focus can flourish, strangers have evolved limited partnerships across former barriers of ethnic-cultural identity, religion, race, language, or rural-urban origins. Such barriers can be outgrown in a variety of settings, including neighborhoods, youth clubs, condominium housing arrangements, citywide school systems, voluntary associations, local-regional churches, and services to immigrants. The chapter closes with a summary of implications, and suggests some lessons learned.

EXERCISES

Common Themes

Identify some common themes in the various coexistence situations described in this chapter. Do these themes give us some clues for overcoming the common forms of resistance to a coexistence way of life?

Taking a Stand

What does coexistence mean for you:
  (a) personally?
  (b) in public places (e.g., where you study, where you work, where you worship, etc.)?
Do you find any connection between your personal stand and the way these organizations or services function?

Promulgating Coexistence

Should the government of your country promote coexistence officially—perhaps by such means as legislation, income tax incentives, or punishments for bigotry? Give some of the reasons underlying your answer.

Preparing Ourselves for Coexistence

What might parents and educators do to lessen our fear of the unknown (which makes those who are different into strangers) or of topics (e.g., such as conflict resolution or coexistence) on which we remain ignorant? Please try to express your suggestions in the first person and on a very practical level.

Chapter 7

From Doubts to Positive Findings

GOOD INTENTIONS ARE NOT ENOUGH

If coexistence is to succeed, it can only happen after most of the people involved have learned how to resolve conflicts, are ready to respect one another's differences, and feel ready to undertake some kind of cooperative activity. To understand how this might come about, and to enable coexistence to progress effectively, the gathering of available research findings (and/or doing some action research ourselves) is essential. We need to know why conflicts erupt, why they escalate, and how to resolve them—especially if we want to reconcile conflicts between ethnic groups (Vasquez, 1995). We also want to learn whatever is known about offering some form of populationwide healing which results in reconciliation and makes subsequent coexistence arrangements possible.

Most practitioners of conflict resolution (and advocates of coexistence) are devoted to their causes and certain about the importance of their efforts. Their impatience to see immediate results, well-intentioned as it may be, is not enough. We also require some sort of disciplined confirmation that their efforts actually produce desired outcomes and do so effectively. In other words, what such activist change agents do or support should be monitored, researched, and evaluated.

RESEARCH MIND-SET

Coexistence outcomes, as well as the resolution of conflicts, can be the result of well-planned projects or can occur spontaneously. Researchers may look at how well a project is prepared, the consumer friendliness of materials and manuals used in orientation sessions, the learning process used to "teach old dogs new tricks," whether the new knowledge is utilized by the learners in their subsequent personal lives or professional practice (both short- and long-term), and whether these efforts spread the word that specific new approaches to coexistence are available (Bjerstedt, 1995).

Many researchers prefer to start with hypotheses, which they try to confirm by gathering data. For example, Stephenson (1982) contended that conflict-resolution efforts work only when the power of the rival parties is balanced. He examined a number of power imbalance cases and compared them to conflicts in which the weaker side had been empowered. The data confirmed his hypothesis.

Similarly, I suggest that when one or both parties in conflict are psychologically or ideologically closed (perhaps out of fear of the unknown), achieving coexistence is very difficult (Chetkow-Yanoov, 1997). Situations of successful coexistence should be analyzed to clarify whether specific efforts (e.g., mediation, economic incentives, healing, education, or nonviolent resistance) had to be made to open up initially closed parties. If the outcome was coexistence, the effectiveness of specific "opening-up" efforts should be evaluated.

Such a combination of creativity, daring, and verified evidence is the backbone of any emerging professional discipline—and is vital to promoting coexistence today.

HELPFUL RESEARCH INDICATORS

Cultural Similarities and Differences

Scholars analyzing the dynamics of conflict have observed that the nature of the local culture is significant (Barnes, 1994; Program on Conflict Resolution, 1990; Watson-Gegeo and White, 1990). Resolving conflicts requires different means in a collectivist culture (e.g., native Hawaiians, Bushmen, Canada's First Nations) than in an individualistic one (e.g., United States and most of Europe).

Barnes takes this cultural focus one step further. He reminds us that in the last two decades of this century, most conflicts have been between ethnic groups within nations, not between nations. At the end of the twentieth century, many collectivist cultures (e.g., in the Balkans, Somalia, Cambodia, or Rwanda) seem engaged in a desperate struggle for survival.

In collectivist cultures, dispute resolution requires high participation of the rival parties; their friends, relatives, and elders; as well as some type of third party, in the process of reconciliation. Everyone has an opportunity to speak, and it is common to express empathy to the "misfit." The elders function as facilitators of overall consensus and, being respected members of the community, will know all those involved personally. Major efforts are invested in healing the emotional wounds of the conflict and in restoring positive social relationships. A detailed description of this collectivist style can be seen in the conflict-resolution practices among the Bushman tribes of southern Africa (Ury, 1995).

On the other hand, working in an individualistic culture pushes us into a paradigm shift. Now parties in conflict favor the help of an expert (e.g., a social worker, mediator, lawyer, or arbitrator) rather than encourage grassroots participation, and the guilty party is to be punished. The expert mediator is expected to be neutral toward those using the service. In collectivist cultures, the conflict-resolution process is consensual, while in individualistic cultures it is adversarial. The resolving of a conflict may now require advocacy or taking action against institutional and national "targets" (Rogers, 1965; Soest and Bryant, 1995; Umbreit, 1995).

Further, as electronic communications and globalization make for worldwide homogenization, members of collectivist cultures may feel more and more hard-pressed to preserve their uniqueness. Their accumulated anxiety and anger often lead to violence.

Dator (1990) suggests that such insights are especially significant when trying to resolve conflicts in new immigrant and refugee communities in North America. In these neighborhoods, coexistence might well be enhanced if the formal judicial system were supplemented with a variety of dispute resolution techniques. Interestingly, in a relatively homogeneous poor neighborhood of San Francisco, people chose to handle local disputes by means of community boards. They learned to use trained volunteer mediators and to rely on word-of-mouth communication, adopting a consensual rather than adversarial style of conflict resolution (Shonholz, 1993).

After studying seventy-two specific international disputes, Bercovitch (1989) found that third-party conflict resolution (e.g., mediation) is most likely to succeed when the following conditions exist:

- The dispute is long, very complex, and increasingly expensive.
- The adversaries' identities are clear and legitimate.
- Cultural or ideological differences are minimal.
- The adversaries (being of equal strength) have reached an impasse.
- Neither side wants further escalation of the dispute.
- Agreements reached can be monitored and enforced.

Bercovitch assumes that real-life mediation, to appreciate the complexity of most conflict situations, should be based on familiarity with systems analysis and be highly empirical in focus. His findings, and those cited previously, give us useful clues on how to move former adversaries toward a coexistence life-style in today's increasingly pluralistic societies.

Basic Needs in Different Cultures

Many scholars, as well as practitioners from the helping professions, have written about the importance of recognizing and satisfying basic human needs (Avruch and Black, 1990; Maslow, 1954; Thursz and Vigilante, 1975; Towle, 1965). Some of them have also come to a related insight—that the achievement of intergroup peace depends on how well we cope with poverty, hunger, illness, humiliation, and ignorance (i.e., unmet basic human needs). All over the world, people who are constantly hungry, whose life-expectancy is thirty-five years, who are exploited or oppressed, and who no longer look to the future with hope are likely to become embroiled in domestic violence or intergroup wars (Lee, 1954; Program on Conflict Resolution, 1990). Fighting is always likely when frustration levels are high and people feel hopeless.

In African countries such as Angola, Botswana, Lesotho, Malawi, or Zimbabwe, social and economic development is seen as the key to preventing conflict. Food and a job (rather than hunger or living in the streets) contribute to social and political stability. Empowerment and increased grassroots participation in decision making are equally vital to gaining and maintaining peaceful coexistence between ethnically different peoples (Nyong'o, 1986).

Are Bicultural Meetings Effective?

One of the most severe separations in Israel is between orthodox religious and secular Jews. Official adult relations are characterized by tension, value-based conflicts, and even violence. Secular and religious Israeli children attend completely segregated public schools—so that they continue to live in competitive separate worlds.

Nevertheless, two religious-secular coexistence projects are flourishing, and they provide us with many indications of effectiveness. In 1995, for example, the Keshet kindergarten and elementary school in Jerusalem set up a deliberate project to bring religious and secular Jewish children together to nurture coexistence within public school classrooms. In a similar vein, a voluntary association called Gesher (bridge) has been holding three, half-day seminars for secular and religious Jewish seventeen-year-olds since 1988.

Both these reports stress how frequent social contacts among peers, and joint learning activities, allow the children to know the "other" as a human being (whose differentness is not threatening) as well as to retain their identity and group affiliation. The pupils and the teaching staff come from both groups, so that all children experience both religious and secular contents and teaching styles. In many cases, parents become part of the project, supporting the pluralism/coexistence experiences of their children (Gordon, 1991; Hirschberg, 1998).

Other Group Processes for Reconciliation

Although this process is not simple or easy, exposure to diverse social realities can eliminate ignorance, counteract fear, and produce tolerance for others "not like me"—which is the essence of coexistence. Many scholars have written about the importance of organized contacts for shifting from segregation and bias to peaceful relations, but do not tempt the participants to depart from their original ethnic/religious tradition (Amir, 1969).

Scholars also underscore that to be successful, single intergroup meetings or ongoing workshops should be held in a place where it is safe to experiment, to make mistakes, and to develop necessary new skills by practicing them anonymously. A lack of immediate deadlines allows enough time for full processes of communication and healing. As the participants get to know and trust one another, no one is excluded, and shame or embarrassment are replaced by taking responsibility for one's own statements and actions. Rather than deny complex issues, they are faced together (Kahn, 1997).

Workshop versions of group activities have also been found effective in resolving long-lasting conflicts. In such continuing group meetings, participants share experiences and perspectives, eventually enabling them to solve problems and resolve conflicts collaboratively. Workshop participants have been observed to undergo personal transformations—becoming able to perceive the needs and fears of the other side or opening up to new ideas. They even become able to plan how to disseminate workshop recommendations in their own and in one another's home countries (Kelman, 1993; Kelman and Rouhana, 1994). Similar processes were helpful in achieving reconciliation between the French and the Germans after World War II (Ackermann, 1994).

Similar findings are characteristic of sophisticated efforts to establish coexistence between Israeli Arabs and Jews. In addition to the report on Neve Shalom in the previous chapter of this book, two daring academics have been creating dialogue between religious Jewish university students and Islamic/Christian students from a variety of Palestinian universities. Under their leadership, religious beliefs and customs were turned into a bridge between the two groups (Mollov and Barhoun, 1997). Discovering commonalities in two religious cultures (in formal circle discussions as well as informally over refreshments) made mutual respect and new friendships possible.

In fact, group experiences such as those just mentioned, when planned and implemented sensitively, often enable a healing process to take place. Gradually, participants feel safe enough to abandon absolutist stands and prejudices to really listen to what other participants are saying, confident enough to admit strong feelings (such as fear or anger) rather than take refuge behind intellectual discussions, and free enough to engage in dialogue rather than in competitive debating or lecturing. After such a group-based healing experience, blaming and self-justification shifts to discovering a shared vision and working as partners to achieve a more desirable future (Kelman, 1991; Montville, 1993; Stauffer, 1987).

Effectiveness of Mediation

Studies show that, in most cases, mediation is more effective than court processes. It consumes less time, reduces costs to both plaintiffs and defendants, raises the contenders' levels of satisfaction, and often makes offender-victim reconciliation possible (Program of Conflict Resolution, 1990; Umbreit and Coates, 1992; Severson and Bankston, 1995). Since mediation requires a high degree of active participation by all parties in the dispute, it has been found very effective in situations of domestic violence and divorce proceedings (Chandler, 1990). Mediation can deal effectively with legally complex cases, and it results in a high percentage of satisfactory agreements—especially when it has the backing of local court judges (Lowery, 1989).

Some sources suggest that the mediator's gender makes a difference. On one hand, management-administration writers contend that women who break into what was once an all-male arena are similarly talented, and their performance does not vary significantly according to gender (Fierman, 1990). Other scholars and practitioners of mediation disagree. Women, unlike their male colleagues, tend not to define themselves as professionally neutral, focus more on process and collaboration, and aim for a transformational change rather than simply to obtain an agreement (Harding, 1986; Koopman et al., 1991; Maxwell, 1992; Weingarten and Douvan, 1985).

Further, positive findings are available regarding the outcomes of volunteer peer mediation done in public schools by pupils of various grade levels. A Hawaiian project, for example, found that participants actually improved in such areas as self-confidence, problem solving, listening skills, ability to write acceptable agreements, and general involvement in school activities (Program on Conflict Resolution, 1990).

A study that monitored high school students who chose to volunteer in various services in a community near Boston also showed positive findings. The teenage participants in this project developed a heightened awareness of community needs, became accepting of cultural diversity, earned higher grades, and showed a high interest in attending college (Lawson, 1997). Such a structured learning-service experience seems likely to constitute preparation for coexisting as adults in the twenty-first century (Vriens and Grootscholten, 1997).

Research done in New York State found that citizen volunteers were practicing mediation and arbitration successfully in their home communities. In addition to their own volunteering, they also recruited other volunteers, engaged in training and public relations activities, and supervised the work of other volunteer mediators. This form of participation gave them a high level of satisfaction and motivated long-term commitment on their part, in addition to constituting an important alternative to adversarial ways of coping with local conflicts. In addition to enhancing conflict management, the ten Dispute Resolution Centers in the study's sample served as vehicles for community empowerment and cooperative problem solving (Rogers, 1989).

SOME BASIC FINDINGS

Regarding conflict resolution, certain findings seem well-established by now. The following are some illustrative examples:

1. The contention that mediators should be neutral toward the parties in conflict and the issue to be resolved is no longer widespread. Contemporary scholars and practitioners do advocate objectivity and professionalism (i.e., that the mediator not favor one side in a conflict), but they realize that most media-

tors strongly desire to prevent the escalation or continuation of a conflict. They are hardly neutral when they want to achieve a win-win resolution.

2. Researchers are also confident that actual resolution of conflicts requires that the adversaries be of similar strength or power. It may be necessary to strengthen the weaker side or put clear limitations on the stronger side's use of its resources, if a win-win outcome is to be achieved.

3. Many recommend the use of system analysis and system models in the professional practice of conflict resolution.

4. There is wide consensus that, for peacemaking, empathic listening skills are important and should be cultivated from the earliest ages.

5. Many recommend two additional conflict-resolution techniques—discovering or creating areas of common interests and finding activities that can be done cooperatively (e.g., Arab and Jewish teens working together in a center serving retarded children). Both these efforts create opportunities to get to know one another socially, to discontinue relying on former stereotypes, to trust one another, and to risk taking first steps toward a coexistence lifestyle.

6. Unilateral conciliatory initiatives (especially by a strong party) are increasingly seen as helping us move along the path to reconciliation (Bercovitch, 1989; Chetkow-Yanoov, 1997; Pruitt, 1995; Stephenson, 1982).

Although my analysis lacks any measurements of statistical correlation, I suggest the following scheme for analyzing complex conflict situations (see Figure 7.1). As we become more sophisticated in coping with the variables suggested previously, the promotion of coexistence should become easier.

Research-based knowledge about topics mentioned in this chapter will no doubt enhance our skills in resolving conflicts, as well as make the attainment of wider coexistence probable.

Figure 7.1. Identifying Some Obstacles to Coexistence

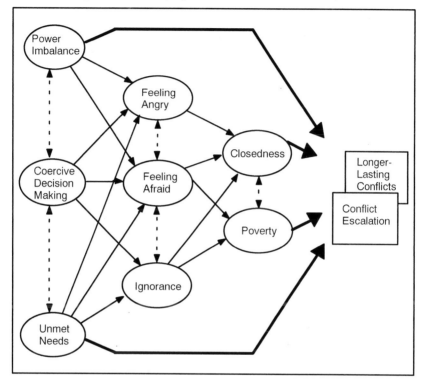

SUGGESTIONS FOR FURTHER RESEARCH

Throughout this chapter, I have assumed that intergroup coexistence becomes possible when appropriate resources are available for managing new disputes as well as for resolving long-lasting ones. If understanding the use of conflict-resolution methods is vital for making coexistence workable, we should know under what conditions human beings seek help in times of trouble.

Available literature (e.g., Aday, Fleming, and Anderson, 1984; Rickwood and Braithwait, 1994) suggests that help-seeking behavior is the outcome of three basic conditions: perception of the difficulty, personal predisposiotions,and enabling factors.

Perception of the Difficulty

It seems relevant to be able to determine whether those experiencing trouble are ready to admit that they require help. This is no doubt connected to whether they perceive their problem subjectively or objectively. Do they have to cope with unmet (internal) needs or with lack of relevant services in their environment? Does their suffering originate from internal distress or from an external threat? At what level of discomfort, say, regarding a feud between neighbors, are they likely to shift from "business as usual" to a readiness to accept outside help?

Personal Predispositions

We may also benefit from having tools to connect some of these considerations to the (cultural- or gender-based) values and norms of those experiencing the trouble. Does the admission of being in trouble produce feelings of shame or of guilt—or is the situation blamed on others? Is the situation accompanied by anger, fear, or a large measure of ignorance? We have to know whether requiring help (again with an interethnic neighborhood conflict) will be interpreted as bravery or as a blow to one's self-esteem, before progress toward coexistence can be made.

Enabling Factors

Resolving conflicts (to make coexistence possible) is directly connected to the existence of relevant help in the sufferer's vicinity. Can the sufferer pay the costs of such help? Are there incentives in the environment that help motivate people to seek and to use help, or does accepting help result in a loss of freedom of action? How much will using help be enhanced by the availability of a support group of colleagues or peers?

It would be useful to know more about factors that move conflicted persons or organizations to admit that their condition is serious, and to seek help for resolving it.

SUMMARY

This chapter argues that we should improve our conflict-resolution skills to help former enemies respect each other's differences and finally live together in a coexistence society. Even if we are not equipped to do research ourselves, we can become sophisticated consumers of available research findings—both to understand conflict situations more accurately and to increase the effectiveness of our intervention efforts.

For example, we could benefit from improved understanding about why conflicts break out and why some of them escalate into violence. We might also inquire into the most appropriate intervention for different types of conflict situations—for example, to practice conflict resolution within different cultures, in relation to meeting various basic human needs, or for getting the participation of diverse personality types. Also, by examining outcomes, we might increase our confidence in the effectiveness of diverse kinds of interventions (e.g., encounter meetings, healing and/or support groups, mediation, or the use of incentives). Eventually, we should be able to pose our own hypotheses about some of these interventions, and learn how to gather data that might confirm or disprove them.

EXERCISES

Doing Research Ourselves

Based on your experience, pose a conflict-resolution idea or issue worth researching, put the basic concepts into operation, make a hypothesis about the relationships you expect to find, and suggest what kind of data you require to confirm or disprove your hypothesis.

How to Combat Ignorance

How would you design an encounter experience between two feuding tribal clans (or cohesive ethnic groups) in a collectivist society? Would you do things differently if the feud was between two groups in an individualistic culture?

Using Biblical Precedents in the Twenty-First Century

How would you explain the biblical injunction to "seek peace and pursue it" to sophisticated pupils in a junior high school of today? Make your explanation very pragmatic and open to empirical evaluation of outcomes as "successful."

Evaluating the Use of Authority for Resolving a Conflict

What would you ask a research consultant if you wanted to try using authority figures (e.g., a respected clergyman/woman, a uniformed police officer, or a popular politician) to resolve a long-standing conflict between two neighborhoods? What kind(s) of research findings would convince your supervisor that this effort had been successful?

Chapter 8

Implications

A REVIEW OF ESTABLISHMENT- MINORITY RELATIONS

As discussed previously, four patterns of intergroup relations have emerged over many centuries of human history. Key to modeling these relations are the extent to which each population group is open-minded and the relative power resources each group commands. When, for the purpose of analysis, these two variables are divided into high-low dichotomies, we can work with a four-fold typology of possible interactions (see Table 8.1).

TABLE 8.1. A Typology of Establishment-Minority Relations

Actual Power Arrangements	Ideology of Participants	
	Flexible and Inclusive	**Closed and Exclusive**
No Unit Has a Monopoly (.5/.5)	1. COEXISTENCE Participation of equals Cooperation based in consensus (e.g., Switzerland)	3. DISAGREEMENT Reluctant collaboration Compromises within turbulence (e.g., South Africa)
One Unit Has a Monopoly (1/0)	2. INTEGRATION Attempts to persuade Accept some loss in favor of greater gains (e.g., United States)	4. SEGREGATION Submission based on coercion Clash normatively or violently (e.g., the Kurds in Turkey)

Segregation

The closed ideology and power monopoly of many historical kings, fanatic religious leaders, or political dictators (often designated "the establishment") usually lead to segregation, oppression, or outright victimization of those defined as outsiders. Usually the minority populations submit to the dictates of such an establishment. However, continuing black-white tensions in Los Angeles or Kurd-Turk skirmishes in the Middle East suggest that if the currently weaker party refuses to submit ideologically the cost of maintaining conformity in the teeth of increasingly violent disagreement *escalates.* All too often, the outcome is a cycle of rebellion and backlash.

This type of reciprocal violence becomes very costly to all the parties embroiled in such a dispute. Exclusion and oppression seem to lead inevitably to violent efforts to get rid of the other "unworthy" party. The outcome is exclusion from, rather than participation in, the overall community, tending to make coexistence unfeasible.

In conflict situations of this type, buffer organizations (e.g., peacekeepers of the United Nations) may be sent to separate the angry disputants. Sometimes, as in the disagreement between the United States and Iran, sanctions will be used to penalize one party. In most such situations, a long process of healing and reconciliation will have to precede any meaningful resolution of the conflict (Chetkow-Yanoov, 1997).

Disengagement

When all parties have similar power capacities, a closed ideology creates the turbulence of disagreement (a modality typical of times of rapid social change). Thus, in South Africa, some white conservatives are still upset about the dismantling of apartheid, and black tribes in Rwanda are still settling scores from earlier times. At some point, with professional help, such adversaries may find it worthwhile to show some readiness for compromises and acts of tolerance—in order to de-escalate from a mutually destructive conflict.

Past enemies may be able to attend formal encounter meetings and, with the help of professional arbitrators and mediators, discover that the stereotypes and biases of former generations are not accurate. As they overcome past suffering and forgive former enemies, they may even become able to move toward a non-adversary form of democratic government (Mansbridge, 1980).

Integration

An open ideology and power monopoly create a situation in which the strong party motivates or "persuades" the others to accept its definition of integration. When such a policy prevails, the weaker parties go through a melting-pot or pressure-cooker experience. They take comfort in knowing that, although other options are available, becoming like the establishment has some short-term benefits. The issue of integration is particularly relevant when large groups of refugees or immigrants have to be absorbed into the host population (as was typical of Irish, Italian, and Jewish immigrant groups who came to the United States during the past century). Fund allocators and teachers are the usual implementers of integration.

Coexistence

Inclusiveness and power balance tend to produce an environment of consensus and participation (elaborated in the next part of this chapter). After normal processes of debating, questioning, or arguing, the conflict-resolution outcome obtained is considered worthwhile by all parties. Open or two-way communications tend to minimize risks, encourage initiative taking, and enhance cooperation. The working together of diverse language-culture cantons in Switzerland or of racial groups in Hawaii serve as pragmatic examples of coexistence.

In general, coexistence is enhanced by exchanges of knowledge or resources between parties who treat each other as equals. When initial conditions are negative, the use of facilitators and mediators is helpful—their goal being to help potential adversaries talk and listen to each other directly. Dialoguing skills, essential for reaching consensus or coexistence, also constitute a basis of real democracy.

PARTICIPATION AND COEXISTENCE

Degrees of citizen participation have been considered essential in definitions of community (Greenberg, 1974; Perlman, 1976), in city planning (Arenstein, 1969; Hollnsteiner, 1977) and in urban renewal (Rossi and Dentter, 1961; Perlman, 1976; Wilson, 1966). As has been mentioned throughout this text, the concept of participation is also essential for an understanding of coexistence.

Usually, participation ensures that all persons who are to be affected by an activity or decision have an opportunity to consider options and to choose among them before something is decided or implemented. Participation calls for decentralized administrative structures—deliberately involving grassroots actors as well as representatives of the power structure in flexible forms of power sharing. Of course, when a participatory process produces a decision, resources must be committed to its implementation.

Participation can produce a sense of belonging or identity, commitment to shared norms or social institutions, a willingness to take responsibility for others, and a readiness for sharing and cooperation. Such outcomes, usually possible among kin and close friends, should also be available in such secondary settings as schools, places of work, religious groups, recreational settings, and branches of governmental services. Actual participation transforms coercive control of dependents into relationships of self-reliance, trust, and partnership.

The achievement of a coexistence society therefore hinges on our readiness to work with people and on the sophistication of our techniques for involving others (rather than doing things for them or in their stead). Actually, achieving participation requires the simultaneous juggling of at least three balls: what purpose will the participation serve, who should be invited to take part, and what are the most appropriate techniques for ensuring that the participation takes place effectively? For example, to survey available knowledge, an interdisciplinary committee of experts might be effective, or neighborhood activists might constitute the best way to learn about local unmet needs (Chetkow-Yanoov, 1986). On the other hand, when a participatory citizen effort gives rise to a new city ordinance, implementation might well be left in the hands of experienced bureaucrat-administrators.

Moreover, when people lack experience in participating in committee meetings, we may have to make special efforts to attract them to come to meetings, as well as to teach them relevant skills (such as the art of listening, keeping minutes, using available data sources, publicity, cooperation, coordination, or negotiating a compromise). Knowing how to participate may, indeed, be essential for citizens to give up defensive behaviors and to dare to coexist with people whom they once found strange or threatening.

A FINAL NOTE

It seems appropriate to conclude this book with excerpts from a short article written by Robert Fulghum (1987):

Most of what I really need to know about how to live, and how to be, I learned in kindergarten. . . . Share. Play fair. Don't hit people. Put things back where you found them. Clean up your own mess. Don't take things that aren't yours. Say you're sorry when you hurt somebody. . . . Live a balanced life. . . . When you go out into the world, watch for traffic, hold hands and stick together. Be aware of wonder. . . . Think what a better world it would be if . . . as nations, we had a basic policy of always putting things back where we found them and cleaning up our own messes. And it is still true, no matter how old you are, when you go out into the world, it is best to hold hands and stick together. (p. 147)

The advantages of coexistence over segregation and integration are well described in this passage. Such a society will probably be characterized by a minimum of conflicts and an absence of violence.

References

Abraham Fund, The (1992). Introduction. *The Abraham Fund Directory,* i-viii.

Abraham Fund delegates meet with Israel's Bedouin community. (1977). *The Abraham Fund Quarterly,* 4(1), Winter, 1 and 6.

Ackermann, A. (1994). Reconciliation as a peace-building process in postwar Europe: The Franco-German case. *Peace and Change,* 19(3), 229-250.

Aday, L. A., Fleming, G. V., and Anderson, R. (1984). *Access to Medical Care in the U.S.A.* Chicago: Pluribus Press.

Alinsky, S. D. (1946). *Reville for Radicals.* Chicago: University of Chicago Press.

Amir, Sharon, S. and Ben-Ari, R. (1984). *School Desegregation: Cross-Cultural Perspectives.* Hillsdale, NJ: Lawrence Erlbaum Associates.

Amir, Y. (1969). Contact hypothesis in ethnic relations. *Psychological Bulletin,* 71, 319-342.

Anda, D. (1984). Bicultural socialization: Factors affecting the minority experience. *Social Work,* 29, March-April, 101-107.

Antonovsky, A. (1960). Identity, anxiety, and the Jew. In *Identity and Anxiety.* Eds. M. Stein, A. J. Vidich, and D. M. White. Glencoe, IL: The Free Press, 428-434.

Arenstein, S. R. (1969). A ladder of citizen participation. *Journal of the American Institute of Planners,* 35, July, 216-224.

Avruckh, K. and Black, P. W. (1990). Ideas of human nature in contemporary conflict resolution theory. *Negotiation Journal,* 6(3), 221-228.

Barnes, B. E. (1994). Conflict resolution across cultures. *Mediation Quarterly,* 12(2), 117-133.

Baumann, M. (1993). The media as mediators. *Conflict Resolution Notes,* 11(2), September, 23-24.

Benedict, R. (1970). Synergy. *Psychology Today,* 4(1), June, 53-56.

Bercovitch, J. (1989). International dispute mediation: A comparative empirical analysis. In *Mediation Research.* Eds. K. Kressel and D. G. Pruitt. San Francisco: Jossey-Bass, 284-299.

Bjerstedt, A. (1995). Schooling for peace in Sweden. *Peace, Environment, and Education,* 6(19), 25-39.

Boulding, E. (1988). Image and action in peace building. *Journal of Social Issues,* 44(2), 17-37.

Brager, G. E. (1968). Advocacy and political behavior. *Social Work,* 13, April, 5-15.

Brager, G. E. and Jarin, V. (1969). Bargaining: A Method in Community Change. *Social Work,* 14, October, 73-83.

Cardozo, A. (1996). Multiculturalism policy works, warts and all. *The Toronto Star,* October 14, A-11.

Chandler, D. (1990). Violence, fear, and communication: The variable impact of domestic violence on mediation. *Mediation Quarterly,* 7(4), 331-346.

Charney, I. (1990). Children of victims and victimizers. *Contemporary Family Therapy,* 12, October, 407-426.

Chetkow, B. (1968). So go fight city hall. In *Neighborhood Organization for Community Action.* Ed. J. B. Turner. New York: National Association of Social Workers, 194-203.

Chetkow-Yanoov, B. (1984). Social work and social action: Implications for the agency. *Habitat International,* 8, 127-139.

————— (1985). *The Pursuit of Peace—A Curriculum Manual for Junior and Senior High School Teachers.* Haifa: Partnership.

————— (1986). Participation as a means to community cooperation. In *Community and Cooperatives in Participatory Development.* Eds. Y. Levi and H. Litwin. Aldershot, England: Gower, 21-35.

————— (1996). Conflict resolution skills can be taught. *Peabody Journal of Education,* 71(3), 12-28.

————— (1997). *Social Work Approaches to Conflict Resolution.* Binghamton, NY: The Haworth Press.

Chetkow-Yanoov, B. and Nadler, S. (1978). Community social workers and political leaders in municipal settings in Israel. *Journal of Social Service Research,* 1(4), Summer, 357-372.

Chin, R. and Benne, K. D. (1969). General strategies for effective changes in human services. In *The Planning of Change,* Second Edition. Eds. W. G. Bennis, K. D. Benne, and R. Chin. New York: Holt, Rinehart and Winston, 32-59.

Clark, M. E. (1990). Meaningful social bonding as a universal human need. In *Conflict: Human Needs Theory.* Ed. J. Burton. London: Macmillan Press, 34-59.

Cornelius, H. and Faire, S. (1989). *Everyone Can Win.* Australia: Simon and Schuster.

Couwenberg, S. W. (1997). The Netherlands has been a multicultural society for ages. *De Volkskrant* (The People's Newspaper), December 3, 8.

Cox, F. M. and Garvin, C. (1970). The relation of social forces to the emergence of community organization practice. In *Strategies of Community Organization.* Eds. F. M. Cox et al. Itasca, IL: Peacock Press, 37-53.

Cracknell, N. (1994). Towards a theology of pluralism. *Current Dialogue,* June, 10-22.

Danieli, Y. (1985). The treatment and prevention of long-term effects of victimization. In *Trauma and Its Wake: The Study and Treatment of Post-Traumatic Disorders.* Ed. C. R. Figley. New York: Brunner/Mazel, 295-313.

Dator, J. (1990). The future of culturally-appropriate ADR. Paper for conference, The Future of the Courts, San Antonio, TX, May 20.

de Haas, N. (1996). Building conflict-resolving government. *Conflict Resolution Network Newsletter.* Chattswood (NSW), Australia, August 1996, 3-9.

Dluhy, M. J. (1990). *Building Coalitions in the Human Services.* Beverly Hills, CA: Sage Publications.

Dominelli, L. (1988). *Anti-Racist Social Work.* London: Macmillan Education Ltd. (and the British Association of Social Workers).

Draft Report of the Work Group on Multiculturalism (1975). Toronto: Board of Education, May 20.

Eaton, J. (1952). Controlled acculturation: A survival technique. *American Sociological Review,* 17, June, 331-340.

Education of Black Students In Toronto Schools (1988). Toronto: Board of Education, May.

Eisler, R. (1987). *The Chalice and the Blade.* San Francisco: Harper & Row.

Erikson, E. H. (1968). *Identity, Youth and Crisis.* New York: W. W. Norton.

Fattah, E. A. (1981). Becoming a victim. *Victimology,* 6(1), 29-47.

Fierman, J. (1990). Do women manage differently? *Fortune,* December 17, 71-74.

Foa, E. B. and Foa, U. G. (1980). Resource theory: Interpersonal behavior as exchange. In *Social Exchange.* Eds. K. J. Gergen, M. S. Greenberg, and R. H. Willis. New York: Plenum Press, 77-94.

Forrest, J. B. (1994). Namibia—The first postapartheid democracy. *Journal of Democracy,* 5(3), 88-100.

Friedman, H. (1997). A brew to battle despair (in South Africa). *The Jerusalem Report,* November 13, 62-66.

Friesen, J. W. (1993). *When Cultures Clash.* Calgary, Canada: Detselig Enterprises, 31-56.

Fromm, E. (1941). *Escape from Freedom.* New York: Holt, Rinehart, and Winston.

Fulghum, R. (1987). We learned it all in kindergarden (condensed from the *Kansas City Times*). *Reader's Digest,* November, 147.

Gibb, J. R. (1978). *Trust: A New View of Personal and Organizational Development.* Los Angeles: Guild of Tutlors Press.

Gordon, C. R. (1991). An evaluation of the Gesher seminars. Paper presented at The First International Conference on Prejudice, Discrimination, and Conflict, July, Jerusalem.

Green, N. S. (1990). *The Giraffe Classroom.* Cleveland Heights, OH: Center for Nonviolent Communication.

Greenberg, M. (1974). A concept of community. *Social Work,* 19, January, 64-72.

Grier, W. H. and Cobbs, P. M. (1968). *Black Rage.* New York: Basic Books.

Gurr, T. R. (1993). *Minorities at Risk.* Washington, DC: United States Institute of Peace Press.

Hardcastle, D. A., Wencour, S., and Powers, P. R. (1997). *Community Practice.* New York: Oxford University Press.

Harding, S. (1986). *The Science Question in Feminism.* Ithaca, NY: Cornell University Press.

Harkabi, Y. (1972). Hostility and the concept of the enemy. *Arab Attitudes to Israel.* Jerusalem: Israel University Press, 113-170.

Harris, I. M. (1988). *Peace Education.* London: McFarland.

Harris, T. G. (1970). About Ruth Benedict and her lost manuscript. *Psychology Today,* 4, June, 51-55, 75-77.

Hayes, K. and Mickelson, J. (1991). *Effecting Change: Social Workers in the Political Arena.* New York: Longman.

Heath, A. (1976). *Rational Choice and Social Exchange: A Critique of Exchange Theory.* New York: Cambridge University Press.

Hirschberg, P. (1998). A study in coexistence. *The Jerusalem Report,* February 19, 26-27.

Hofer, M. (1997). Grass roots connections: 4-H renews its mission by cultivating diversity. *Teaching Tolerance,* Spring, 41-45.

Hoffer, E. (1951). *The True Believer.* New York: Harper & Row.

Hoffman, J.E. (1982). Social identity and the readiness for social relations between Jews and Arabs in Israel. *Human Relations,* 35, 727-741.

Hollnsteiner, M. R. (1977). People power: Community participation in the planning of human settlements. *Assignment Children (UNICEF),* 40, October, 11-47.

Holmes, M. (1992). *Education Policy for Pluralist Democracy.* Washington, DC: The Palmer Press.

Hume, J. (1993). A new Ireland in a new Europe. In *Northern Ireland and the Politics of Reconciliation.* Eds. D. Keogh and M. H. Haltzel. New York: Cambridge University Press, 226-233.

Hunter, F. (1953). *Community Power Structure.* Chapel Hill, NC: University of North Carolina Press.

Jabri, V. (1990). *Mediating Conflicts: Decision Making and Western Intervention in Namibia.* New York: Manchester University Press.

Jones, M. (1991). It's a not so small world. *Newsweek,* September 9, 42-43.

Kahn, S. (1997). Multiracial organizations: Theory and practice. The Union Institute. *Network,* 14(2), 27-29.

Kalmakoff, S. and Shaw, J. (1987). *Peer Conflict Resolution Through Creative Negotiation: A Curriculum for Grades 4 to 6.* New Westminster, Canada: Public Education for Peace Society (PEPS).

Kelman, H. C. (1987). The political psychology of the Israeli-Palestinian conflict. *Political Psychology,* 8, 347-363.

_____ (1991). Interactive problem solving: The uses and limits of a therapeutic model for the resolution of international conflicts. In *Psychodynamics of International Relationships,* Volume II. Eds. V. D. Volkan, J. V. Montiolle, and D. A. Julius. Lexington, MA: Lexington Books, 145-160.

_____ (1993). Coalitions across conflict lines. In *Conflict Between People and Groups.* Eds. S. Worchel and J. Simpson. Chicago: Nelson-Hall, 236-258.

Kelman, H. C. and Rouhana, N. N. (1994). Promoting joint thinking in international conflicts: An Israeli-Palestinian continuing workshop. *Journal of Social Issues,* 50(1), 157-178.

Kettner, P. M., Daley, J. M., and Nichols, A. W. (1985). *Initiating Changes in Organizations and Communities.* Monterey, CA: Brooks/Cole (Wadsworth).

Kleyman, P. (1974). *Senior Power: Growing Up Rebelliously.* San Francisco: Glide Publications.

Koopman, E., Hunt, E., Favrett, F., Coltri, L., and Britten, T. (1991). Professional perspectives on court-connected child custody mediation. *Family and Conciliation Courts Review,* 29, 301-317.

Kornblum, S. and Lieberman, C. A. (1975). Institutionalization of political action among senior adults in a community center. *Journal of Jewish Community Service,* 51, Spring, 251-259.

Kosmin, B. (1979). Exclusion and opportunity. In *Ethnicity at Work.* Ed. S. Wallman. London: Macmillan, 37-68.

Kronish, R. (1997). Understanding one another in Israel. *Brandeis Review,* Spring, 19-23.

Kung, S. W. (1962). *Chinese in American Life.* Seattle, WA: University of Washington Press.

Lawson, E. (1997). Learn and serve (as a volunteer). *Brandeis Review,* Fall, 48-49.

Lee, D. (1959). Are basic needs ultimate? In *Freedom and Culture.* New York: Spectrum Books (Prentice-Hall), 70-77.

Lee, T. (1954). *In the Cause of Peace: Seven Years with the United Nations.* New York: Macmillan.

Lewin, K. (1948). Self-hatred among Jews. In *Resolving Social Conflicts.* New York: Harper, 186-200.

Lewis, R. G. and Keung, M. (1975). Social work with Native Americans. *Social Work,* 20, September, 379-382.

Lingas, L. G. (1988). Conflict resolution within family and community networks. *Nordic Journal of Social Work,* 8, 48-58.

Lipsky, R. (1968). Protest as a political resource. *American Political Science Review,* 62, December, 1144-1158.

Lowery, K. (1989). *Mediation of Complex and Public Interest Cases: An Evaluation Report.* Honolulu: Program on Conflict Resolution of the University of Hawaii.

Lyon, M. (1997). A place to start. *Brandeis Review,* 17(2), Winter, 32-36.

Mansbridge, J. J. (1980). *Beyond Adversary Democracy.* New York: Basic Books.

Maranz, F. (1993). Bridging the gulf. *The Jerusalem Reporter,* April 22, 28-29.

Martinez, B. (1997). Unite and overcome! *Teaching Tolerance,* Spring, 11-15.

Maslow, A. H. (1954). *Motivation and Personality.* New York: Harper & Row.

——————— (1968). *Towards a Psychology of Being,* Second Edition. New York: Van Nostrand.

Maxwell, D. (1992). Gender differences in mediation style and their impact on mediator effectiveness. *Mediation Quarterly,* 9(4), 353-364.

McCann, J. E. and Gray, B. (1986). Power and collaboration in the human service domains. *International Journal of Sociology and Social Policy,* 6, 58-76.

McMahon, A. and Allen-Meares, P. (1992). Is social work racist? A content analysis of recent literature. *Social Work,* 37(6), November, 533-539.

Mindell, A. (1995). Revenge and cultural transformation. *Sitting in the Fire.* Portland, OR: Lao Tse Press, 75-88.

Mitchell, C. (1990). Necessitous man and conflict resolution. In *Conflict: Human Needs Theory.* Ed. J. Burton. London: Macmillan, 149-176.

Mollov, B. and Barhoun, M. I. (1997). Building cultural bridges between Arab and Jewish university students. <http://www.ariga.com/peacebiz/edits/bridges.htm>

Montville, J. V. (1989). *Conflict and Peacemaking in Multi-Ethnic Societies.* Lexington, MA: Lexington Books.

———— (1993). The healing function in political conflict resolution. In *Conflict Resolution: Healing and Practice.* Eds. D. J. Sandole and H. van der Merwe. Manchester University Press, 112-127.

Moran, B. (1992). *A Little Rebellion.* Vancouver, BC: Arsenal Pulp Press.

Nathan, L. (1992). The trials of reconciliation in Namibia. *Track-Two,* 1(3), 1-4.

Netting, F. E., Kettner, P. M., and McMurty, S. L. (1993). *Social Work Macropractice.* New York: Longman.

Neve Shalom Newsletter, May-August 1992, April-October 1993, November 1995, September 1996, January 1998.

Nyong'o, P. A. (1986). An African perspective on peace and development. *International Social Science Journal,* 110, 575-588.

Percy, C. H. (1974). *Growing Old in the Country of the Young.* New York: McGraw Hill.

Peres, Y. and Shemer, S. (1984). The ethnic factor in the elections of the tenth Knesset. *Migamot,* 18, March, 316-331, in Hebrew.

Perlman, J. E. (1976). Grassrooting the system. *Social Policy,* 7, September-October, 4-20.

Poort-van Eeden, J. (1997). Coexistence activities in Holland. Haarlem: Overleggroep Mondiale Vorming (OMVo), April, unpublished report.

Pray, K. L. M. (1947). When is community organization social work practice? *Proceedings, National Conference of Social Work.* New York: Columbia University Press.

Program on Conflict Resolution (1990). *Researching Disputes Across Cultures and Institutions.* Manoa, HI: University of Hawaii.

Pruitt, D. G. (1995). The psychology of social conflict and its relevance to international conflict. In *Beyond Confrontation.* Eds. J. A. Vasquez, J. T. Johnson, S. Jaffe, and L. Stamato. Ann Arbor, MI: University of Michigan Press, 103-114.

Purnell, D. (1988). Creative conflict. *WCCI Forum,* 2, June, 30-52.

Rich, Y., Amir, Y. and Ben-Ari, R. (1981). Social and emotional problems associated with integration in the Israeli junior high schools. *International Journal of Inter- Cultural Relations,* 5, 259-275.

Rickwood, D. J. and Braithwait, V. A. (1994). Social-psychological factors affecting help-seeking for emotional problems. *Social Science Medicine,* 39(4), 563-572.

Rogers, C. R., Kanrich, S., and Steinhauser, I. (1965). Dealing with psychological tensions. *Journal of Applied Behavioural Science,* 1, January-March, 6-24.

Rogers, S. J. (1989). *Understanding Our Criminal Justice Volunteers.* New York: Brooklyn Mediation Center.

Rosenberg, M. B. (1983). *A Model for Nonviolent Communication.* Philadelphia: New Society Publishers.

Ross, M. and Lappin, B. W. (1967). The role of the professional worker. In *Community Organization.* New York: Harper & Row, 203-231.

Rossi, P. H. and Dentter, R. A. (1961). *The Politics of Urban Renewal.* New York: Free Press.

Rothman, J. (1970). Three models of community organization. In *Strategies of Community Organization.* Ed. F. M. Fox. Itasca, IL: Peacock Press, 20-36.

_____ (1974). Practitioner roles. In *Planning and Organizing for Social Change.* New York: Columbia University Press, 35-60.

Rothman, J., Erlich, J. L., and Tropman, J. E. (1995). *Strategies of Community Intervention.* Itasca: IL, Peacock Press.

Samooha, S. (1978). *Israel: Pluralism and Conflict.* London: Routledge and Kegan Paul.

_____ (1984). Three perspectives in the sociology of ethnic relations in Israel. *Migamot,* 18, March, 169-206, in Hebrew.

Shonholz, R. (1993). The role of minorities in establishing mediation norms and institutions. *Mediation Quarterly,* 10(3), 231-241.

Severson, M. M. and Bankston, T. V. (1995). Social work and the pursuit of justice through mediation. *Social Work,* 40(5), 683-691.

Shamir, M. and Sullivan, J. L. (1985). Jews and Arabs in Israel: Everybody hates somebody, sometime. *Journal of Conflict Resolution,* 29, June, 283-305.

Shepard, A. C. (1994-1995). Community journalism. *The Responsive Community,* 5, Winter, 30-40.

Shera, W. and Page, J. (1995). Creating more effective human service organizations through strategies of empowerment. *Administration in Social Work,* 19(4), 1-15.

Simon, D. (1993). Namibia's new geopolitics: Lessons for South Africa. *Indicator SA,* 10(4), 73-76.

Sklare, M. (1958). *The Jews: Social Patterns of an American Group.* New York: Free Press.

Snow, C. P. (1960). *Science and Government.* Cambridge, MA: Harvard University Press.

Soest, D. and Bryant, S. (1995). Violence reconceptualized for social work. *Social Work,* 40(4), 549-337.

Sosin, M. and Caulum, S. (1983). Advocacy: A conceptualization for social work practice. *Social Work,* 28(1), 12-17.

Sparks, D. L. and Green, D. (1992). *Namibia: The Nation After Independence.* Boulder, CO: Westview Press.

Specht, H. (1969). Disruptive tactics. *Social Work,* 14, April, 5-15.

Spiegel, F. Z. (1997). How to Hide from Jewish pluralism. *The Jerusalem Report,* September 4, 58.

Stauffer E. R. (1987). *Unconditional Love and Forgiveness.* Burbank, CA: Triangle Publishers.

Stephenson, C. (1982). *Alternative Methods for International Security.* Washington, DC: University Press of America.

Suter, K. D. (1996). The need for a new political culture. *Conflict Resolution Network News* (Australia), 33, August, 11-15, an occasional paper.

Thurz, D. and Vigilante, J. L., Eds. (1975). *Meeting Human Needs: An Overview of Nine Countries,* Volume 1. London: Sage.

Towle, C. (1965). *Common Human Needs.* New York: American Association of Social Workers.

Umbreit, M. S. (1995). *Mediating Interpersonal Conflicts.* West Concord, MN: CPI Publishing.

Umbreit, M. S. and Coates, R. (1992). *Victim-Offender Mediation: An Analysis of Programs in Four States of the U.S.* Minneapolis: Minnesota Citizens Council on Crime and Justice.

Ury, W. L. (1995). Conflict resolution among the Bushmen. *Negotiation Journal,* October, 379-389.

Vasquez, J. A. (1995). The learning of peace: Lessons from a multidisciplinary inquiry. In *Beyond Confrontation.* Eds. J. A. Vasquez, J. T. Johnson, S. Jaffe, and L. Stamato. Ann Arbor, MI: University of Michigan Press, 211-228.

Volkan, V. D. (1985). The need to have enemies and allies. *Political Psychology,* 6, June, 219-247.

Vriens, L. and Grootscholten, J. (1997). Peace education and teaching conflict in school: An action research project. Paper presented at the Third International Education Conference, University of Cincinnati, OH: April 15-20.

Wade, J. C. (1993). Institutional racism: An analysis of the mental health system. *American Journal of Orthopsychiatry,* 63(4), October, 536-544.

Wahlstrom, R. (1989). *Enemy Images and Peace Education.* Malmo, Sweden: School of Education, September, Miniprint No. 660.

Warren, R. L. (1969). Types of purposive change. *Readings in Community Organization.* Eds. R. M. Kramer and H. Specht. Englewood Cliffs, NJ: Prentice-Hall, 205-222.

Watson-Gegeo, K. and White, G. M. (1990). *Disentangling: Conflict Discourse in Pacific Societies.* Stanford, CA: Stanford University Press.

Watts, L. G. and Hughes, H. (1964). Portrait of a self-integrator. *Journal of Social Issues,* April, 103-115.

We Are All Immigrants to This Place: A Look at the Toronto School System in Terms of Multiculturalism (1976). Toronto: Board of Education.

Weingarten, H. R. and Douvan, E. (1985). Male and female visions of mediation. *Negotiation Journal,* 1, October, 349-358.

Weingarten, H. R. and Douvan, E., and Leas, S. (1987). Levels of marital conflict: A guide to assessment and intervention in troubled marriages. *American Journal of Orthopsychiatry,* 57, July, 407-417.

Williams, W. H. A. (1997). Immigration as a pattern in American culture. *The Union Institute Network,* 14(2), Summer, 35-40.

Wilson, J. O. (1966). *Urban Renewal: The Record and the Controversy.* Cambridge, MA: MIT Press.

York, A. S. (1984). Towards a conceptual model of community social work. *British Journal of Social Work,* 14, June, 241-255.

Young, W. M. (1967). The case for urban integration. *Social Work,* 12, July, 12-17.

Yuhui, L. (1996). Neighborhood organization and local social action. *Journal of Community Practice,* 3(1), 35-58.

Zander, A. (1990). Pressuring methods used by groups. In *Effective Social Action by Community Groups.* San Francisco: Jossey-Bass, 125-132, 140-161.

Index

Page numbers followed by the letter "f" indicate figures; those followed by the letter "t" indicate tables.

HAWORTH Social Work Practice
Carlton E. Munson, PhD, Senior Editor

SOCIAL WORK: SEEKING RELEVANCY IN THE TWENTY-FIRST CENTURY by Roland Meinert, John T. Pardeck, and Larry Kreuger. (2000).

SOCIAL WORK PRACTICE IN HOME HEALTH CARE by Ruth Ann Goode. (2000). "Dr. Goode presents both a lucid scenario and a formulated protocol to bring health care services into the home setting. . . . This is a must have volume that will be a reference to be consulted many times." *Marcia B. Steinhauer, PhD, Coordinator and Associate Professor, Human Services Administration Program, Rider University, Lawrenceville, New Jersey*

FORENSIC SOCIAL WORK: LEGAL ASPECTS OF PROFESSIONAL PRACTICE, SECOND EDITION by Robert L. Barker and Douglas M. Branson. (2000). "The authors combine their expertise to create this informative guide to address legal practice issues facing social workers." *Newsletter of the National Organization of Forensic Social Work*

HUMAN SERVICES AND THE AFROCENTRIC PARADIGM by Jerome H. Schiele. (2000). "Represents a milestone in applying the Afrocentric paradigm to human services generally, and social work specifically. . . . A highly valuable resource." *Bogart R. Leashore, PhD, Dean and Professor, Hunter College School of Social Work, New York, New York*

SOCIAL WORK IN THE HEALTH FIELD: A CARE PERSPECTIVE by Lois A. Fort Cowles. (1999). "Makes an important contribution to the field by locating the practice of social work in health care within an organizational and social context." *Goldie Kadushin, PhD, Associate Professor, School of Social Welfare, University of Wisconsin, Milwaukee*

SMART BUT STUCK: WHAT EVERY THERAPIST NEEDS TO KNOW ABOUT LEARNING DISABILITIES AND IMPRISONED INTELLIGENCE by Myrna Orenstein. (1999). "A trailblazing effort that creates an entirely novel way of talking and thinking about learning disabilities. There is simply nothing like it in the field." *Fred M. Levin, MD, Training Supervising Analyst, Chicago Institute for Psychoanalysis; Assistant Professor of Clinical Psychiatry, Northwestern University, School of Medicine, Chicago, IL*

CLINICAL WORK AND SOCIAL ACTION: AN INTEGRATIVE APPROACH by Jerome Sachs and Fred Newdom. (1999). "Just in time for the new millennium come Sachs and Newdom with a wholly fresh look at social work. . . . A much-needed uniting of social work values, theories, and practice for action." *Josephine Nieves, MSW, PhD, Executive Director, National Association of Social Workers*

SOCIAL WORK PRACTICE IN THE MILITARY by James G. Daley. (1999). "A significant and worthwhile book with provocative and stimulating ideas. It deserves to be read by a wide audience in social work education and practice as well as by decision makers in the military." *H. Wayne Johnson, MSW, Professor, University of Iowa, School of Social Work, Iowa City, Iowa*

GROUP WORK: SKILLS AND STRATEGIES FOR EFFECTIVE INTERVEN-TIONS, SECOND EDITION by Sondra Brandler and Camille P. Roman. (1999). "A clear, basic description of what group work requires, including what skills and techniques group workers need to be effective." *Hospital and Community Psychiatry* (from the first edition)

TEENAGE RUNAWAYS: BROKEN HEARTS AND "BAD ATTITUDES" by Laurie Schaffner, (1999). "Skillfully combines the authentic voice of the juvenile runaway with the principles of social science research."

CELEBRATING DIVERSITY: COEXISTING IN A MULTICULTURAL SOCIETY by Benyamin Chetkow-Yanoov. (1999). "Makes a valuable contribution to peace theory and practice." *Ian Harris, EdD, Executive Secretary, Peace Education Committee, International Peace Research Association*

SOCIAL WELFARE POLICY ANALYSIS AND CHOICES by Hobart A. Burch. (1999). "Will become the landmark text in its field for many decades to come." *Sheldon Rahan, DSW, Founding Dean and Emeritus Professor of Social Policy and Social Administration. Faculty of Social Work, Wilfrid Laurier University, Canada*

SOCIAL WORK PRACTICE: A SYSTEMS APPROACH, SECOND EDITION by Benyamin Chetkow-Yannov. (1999). "Highly recommended as a primary text for any and all introductory social work courses." *Ram A. Cnaan, PhD, Associate Professor, School of Social Work, University of Pennsylvania*

CRITICAL SOCIAL WELFARE ISSUES: TOOLS FOR SOCIAL WORK AND HEALTH CARE PROFESSIONALS edited by Arthur J. Katz, Abraham Lurie, and Carlos M. Vidal. (1997). "Offers hopeful agendas for change, while navigating the societal challenges facing those in the human services today." *Book News Inc.*

SOCIAL WORK IN HEALTH SETTINGS: PRACTICE IN CONTEXT, SECOND EDITION edited by Toba Schwaber Kerson. (1997). "A first-class document . . . It will be found among the steadier and lasting works on the social work aspects of American health care." *Hans S. Falck, PhD, Professor Emeritus and Former Chair, Health Specialization in Social Work, Virginia Commonwealth University*

PRINCIPLES OF SOCIAL WORK PRACTICE: A GENERIC PRACTICE APPROACH by Molly R. Hancock. (1997). "Hancock's discussions advocate reflection and self-awareness to create a climate for client change." *Journal of Social Work Education*

NOBODY'S CHILDREN: ORPHANS OF THE HIV EPIDEMIC by Steven F. Dansky. (1997). "Professional sound, moving, and useful for both professionals and interested readers alike." *Ellen G. Friedman, ACSW, Associate Director of Support Services, Beth Israel Medical Center, Methadone Maintenance Treatment Program*

SOCIAL WORK APPROACHES TO CONFLICT RESOLUTION: MAKING FIGHTING OBSOLETE by Benyamin Chetkow-Yanoov. (1996). "Presents an examination of the nature and cause of conflict and suggests techniques for coping with conflict." *Journal of Criminal Justice*

FEMINIST THEORIES AND SOCIAL WORK: APPROACHES AND APPLICA-TIONS by Christine Flynn Salunier. (1996). " An essential reference to be read repeatedly by all educators and practitioners who are eager to learn more about feminist theory and practice: *Nancy R. Hooyman, PhD, Dean and Professor, School of Social Work, University of Washington, Seattle*

THE RELATIONAL SYSTEMS MODEL FOR FAMILY THERAPY: LIVING IN THE FOUR REALITIES by Donald R. Bardill. (1996). "Engages the reader in quiet, thoughtful conversation on the timeless issue of helping families and individuals." *Christian Counseling Resource Review*

SOCIAL WORK INTERVENTION IN AN ECONOMIC CRISIS: THE RIVER COMMUNITIES PROJECT by Martha Baum and Pamela Twiss. (1996). "Sets a standard for universities in terms of the types of meaningful roles they can play in supporting and sustaining communities." *Kenneth J. Jaros, PhD, Director, Public Health Social Work Training Program, University of Pittsburgh*

FUNDAMENTALS OF COGNITIVE-BEHAVIOR THERAPY: FROM BOTH SIDES OF THE DESK by Bill Borcherdt. (1996). "Both beginning and experienced practitioners . . . will find a considerable number of valuable suggestions in Borcherdt's book." *Albert Ellis, PhD, President, Institute for Rational-Emotive Therapy, New York City*

BASIC SOCIAL POLICY AND PLANNING: STRATEGIES AND PRACTICE METHODS by Hobart A. Burch. (1996). "Burch's familiarity with his topic is evident and his book is an easy introduction to the field." *Readings*

THE CROSS-CULTURAL PRACTICE OF CLINICAL CASE MANAGEMENT IN MENTAL HEALTH edited by Peter Manoleas. (1996). "Makes a contribution by bringing together the cross-cultural and clinical case management perspectives in working with those who have serious mental illness." *Disability Studies Quarterly*

FAMILY BEYOND FAMILY: THE SURROGATE PARENT IN SCHOOLS AND OTHER COMMUNITY AGENCIES by Sanford Weinstein. (1995). "Highly recommended to anyone concerned about the welfare of our children and the breakdown of the American family." *Jerold S. Greenberg, EdD, Director of Community Service, College of Health & Human Performance, University of Maryland*

PEOPLE WITH HIV AND THOSE WHO HELP THEM: CHALLENGES, INTEGRATION, INTERVENTION by R. Dennis Shelby. (1995). "A useful and compassionate contribution to the HIV psychotherapy literature." *Public Health*

THE BLACK ELDERLY: SATISFACTION AND QUALITY OF LATER LIFE by Marguerite Coke and James A. Twaite. (1995). "Presents a model for predicting life satisfaction in this population." *Abstracts in Social Gerontology*

BUILDING ON WOMEN'S STRENGTHS: A SOCIAL WORK AGENDA FOR THE TWENTY-FIRST CENTURY edited by Liane V. Davis. (1994). "The most lucid and accessible overview of the related epistemological debates int he social work literature." *Journal of the National Association of Social Workers*

NOW DARE EVERYTHING: TALES OF HIV-RELATED PSYCHOTHERAPY by Steven F. Dansky. (1994). "A highly recommended book for anyone working with persons who are HIV positive. . . . Every library should have a copy of this book." *AIDS Book Review Journal*

INTERVENTION RESEARCH: DESIGN AND DEVELOPMENT FOR HUMAN SERVICE edited by Jack Rothman and Edwin J. Thomas. (1994). "Provides a useful framework for the further examination of methodology for each separate step of such research." *Academic Library Book Review*

CLINICAL SOCIAL WORK SUPERVISION, SECOND EDITION by Carlton E. Munson. (1993). "A useful, thorough, and articulate reference for supervisors and for 'supervisees' who are wanting to understand their supervisor or are looking for effective supervision." *Transactional Analysis Journal*

ELEMENTS OF THE HELPING PROCESS: A GUIDE FOR CLINICIANS by Raymond Fox. (1993). "Filled with helpful hints, creative interventions, and practical guidelines." *Journal of Family Psychotherapy*

IF A PARTNER HAS AIDS: GUIDE TO CLINICAL INTERVENTION FOR RELATIONSHIPS IN CRISIS by R. Dennis Shelby. (1993). " A welcome addition to existing publications about couples coping with AIDS, it offers intervention ideas and strategies to clinicians." *Contemporary Psychology*

GERONTOLOGICAL SOCIAL WORK SUPERVISION by Ann Burack-Weiss and Frances Coyle Brennan. (1991). "The creative ideas in this book will aid supervisors working with students and experienced social workers." *Senior News*

SOCIAL WORK THEORY AND PRACTICE WITH THE TERMINALLY ILL by Joan K. Parry. (1989). "Should be read by all professionals engaged in the provision of health services in hospitals, emergency rooms, and hospices." *Hector B. Garcia, PhD, Professor, San Jose State University School of Social Work*

THE CREATIVE PRACTITIONER: THEORY AND METHODS FOR THE HELPING SERVICES by Bernard Gelfand. (1988). "[Should] be widely adopted by those in the helping services. It could lead to significant positive advances by countless individuals." *Sidney J. Parnes, Trustee Chairperson for Strategic Program Development, Creative Education Foundation, Buffalo, NY*

MANAGEMENT AND INFORMATION SYSTEMS IN HUMAN SERVICES: IMPLICATIONS FOR THE DISTRIBUTION OF AUTHORITY AND DECISION MAKING by Richard K. Caputo. (1987). "A contribution to social work scholarship in that it provides conceptual frameworks that can be used in the design of management information systems." *Social Work*

Order Your Own Copy of
This Important Book for Your Personal Library!

CELEBRATING DIVERSITY
Coexisting in a Multicultural Society

_____ in hardbound at $39.95 (ISBN: 0-7890-0437-2)

_____ in softbound at $14.95 (ISBN: 0-7890-0438-0)

COST OF BOOKS_____	☐ **BILL ME LATER:** ($5 service charge will be added) (Bill-me option is good on US/Canada/Mexico orders only; not good to jobbers, wholesalers, or subscription agencies.)
OUTSIDE USA/CANADA/ MEXICO: ADD 20%_____	
POSTAGE & HANDLING_____ (US: $3.00 for first book & $1.25 for each additional book) Outside US: $4.75 for first book & $1.75 for each additional book)	☐ Check here if billing address is different from shipping address and attach purchase order and billing address information. Signature_____
SUBTOTAL_____	☐ **PAYMENT ENCLOSED:** $_____
IN CANADA: ADD 7% GST_____	☐ **PLEASE CHARGE TO MY CREDIT CARD.**
STATE TAX_____ (NY, OH & MN residents, please add appropriate local sales tax)	☐ Visa ☐ MasterCard ☐ AmEx ☐ Discover Account #_____
FINAL TOTAL_____ (If paying in Canadian funds, convert using the current exchange rate. UNESCO coupons welcome.)	Exp. Date_____ Signature_____

Prices in US dollars and subject to change without notice.

NAME _____

INSTITUTION _____

ADDRESS _____

CITY _____

STATE/ZIP _____

COUNTRY _____ COUNTY (NY residents only) _____

TEL _____ FAX _____

E-MAIL_____

May we use your e-mail address for confirmations and other types of information? ☐ Yes   ☐ No

Order From Your Local Bookstore or Directly From
The Haworth Press, Inc.
10 Alice Street, Binghamton, New York 13904-1580 • USA
TELEPHONE: 1-800-HAWORTH (1-800-429-6784) / Outside US/Canada: (607) 722-5857
FAX: 1-800-895-0582 / Outside US/Canada: (607) 772-6362
E-mail: getinfo@haworthpressinc.com
PLEASE PHOTOCOPY THIS FORM FOR YOUR PERSONAL USE.

BOF96